# TRADING SYSTEM SECRETS

JOE
KRUTSINGER

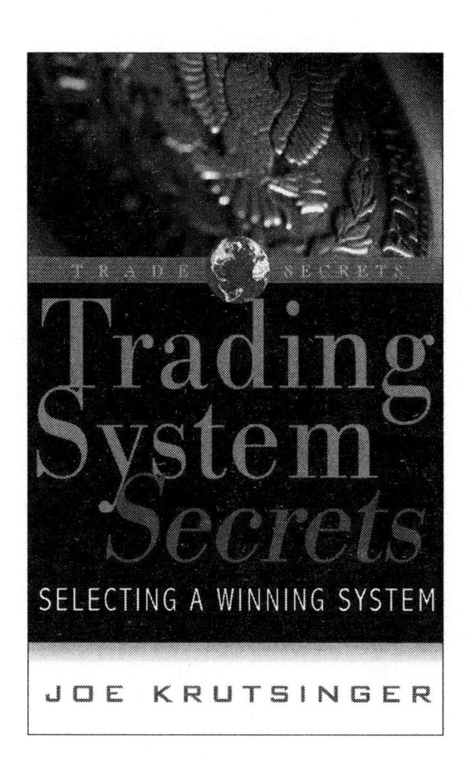
TRADE SECRETS
Trading System Secrets
SELECTING A WINNING SYSTEM
JOE KRUTSINGER

Published by Marketplace Books
Reprinted by arrangement with The McGraw-Hill Companies.



ISBN 1-883272-26-2

*Printed in the United States of America.*

# CONTENTS

# ACKNOWLEDGEMENT

Thanks to my friend and mentor, Larry Williams, who, as far as I know, originated taking a look at "open of tomorrow" on trading systems and rule sets, and who's getting out at a certain "profitable" opening is his unique concept.

I have incorporated these tremendous ideas into trading systems and rule sets that hopefully anyone could appreciate and enjoy. If you look over the simulations of "Bail Suite" in the back of this book, and would like more information, call 1-800-272-2855 extension T184 and I will be glad to give you additional information.

Now, let's take a look at the step-by-step way to select your winning system – *Trading System Secrets* by Joe Krutsinger:

# INTRODUCTION

**IN THE EARLY 1980'S,** I purchased one of the first Macintosh computers. Introduction of the "Mac" signaled the start of a virtual revolution for traders. Back then, before the prevalence of personal computers, the best way to run a trading system was using a spread sheet and typing in a price every fifteen minutes - or whatever your timeframe required - and calculating the relationship between that price and the moving average of that price. An egg timer would be set for the desired time interval and, when the beeper went off, we'd capture the tick in the spreadsheet. This was considered "high-tech" trading system technology at the time - and very successful trading systems were developed using these rudimentary methods.

Obviously, much has changed in the years since. The prevalence of personal computers and the large number of good, affordable software trading programs on the market has provided traders with an increasing array of exciting new tools that allow them to develop better, more profitable trading skills and systems. Several of these programs will be introduced and evaluated in this book.

The internet is also opening doors to all traders, making timely, complex information previously available only to the professionals accessible to the masses. The 'net' is just the latest of the tools revolutionizing the trading landscape. And, like any good carpenter, traders need to continue adding these new tools to their toolbox, so they can perfect their craft - and increase their profits - by using them.

But, much as a carpenter would not attempt to build a house with only a hammer - traders should not venture into the markets armed only with fancy, high-tech programs and a bit of knowledge. New technology can certainly simplify your trading and improve your body of information. But success still lies, in large part, on selecting the right system for you. It's the 'foundation' of your "house," if you will, and system selection is a critical factor in trading success.

There are limitless ways to trade the market. But the top system traders - many of whom I interviewed for my book Trading Systems - have one element in common: They each have found a system that works for them. It suits their temperament, their risk level, their timeframe, and their overall goal structure. Much of this book is devoted to showing you how to pick a system that will accomplish your goals - and give you the opportunity to become a consistently winning trader.

Over the years I've had the privilege of not only interviewing many of the world's greatest system traders, I've been honored to write trading systems for some of them. Some systems have had incredible success - others less so. But I've survived the trading 'battlefield' and have emerged a stronger, wiser trader with new insights into the process and the markets - and much of this I also share with you in the this book in an easy-to-follow, "Q & A" format.

With the advent of new technology that's made trading and system building easier and more effective - it's also true that our lives are busier than ever. Most people today don't want to sit and watch the market - tick by tick. Yet they also have an urge to do more than buy and hold. How to resolve this dilemma? Do they buy a software package that requires them to monitor a computer screen all day? Do they hook it up to a beeper mechanism and hope they don't get a bad tick? Do they stay with end-of-the day data and miss all the action based upon the openings and events that happen overnight? Description of the Bail Suite product I have developed might give traders an another option for resolving this predicament favorably.

Overall, most of what I've learned in trading has come as much from my own experiences - as from observing and learning from the winning ways of successful traders I admire. My friend and mentor Larry Williams is someone from whom I've learned a tremendous amount, and his unique concepts have impacted my own system development. I hope this book will have a similar affect on many of you - and will help you - step-by-step - select a winning trading system.

# SELECTING A WINNING SYSTEM

## EXAMINING OTHERS' APPROACHES

By looking at my first SystemWriter experience, you can get an idea of how to incorporate traditional or other successful approaches into your own system.

The first time I worked on this system was in 1987 when I acquired my first SystemWriter. I was a speaker at one of the Futures Symposiums International in Las Vegas. I was an options guru, a speaker on the platform, and I was doing very well.

A young man came up to me. His name was Bill Cruz, and he was an unknown at the time in the futures business. He is a very smart, good-looking, young, successful guy.

He said, "Mr Krutsinger, I read your book, *The Commodities Cookbook*, and I saw that you had a trading system in there." (I had made the point in my book that it had taken me $300-$400 and three to four months to get the completed track record.) The trading system was: "If the close is above the 32-day moving average in silver, you are long. If it is not, you are short." (See Figures 1, 2, and 3)

Back in those days it was a great system because hardly anybody had this kind of equipment, and moving averages were terrific.

Bill took me over to a booth with no signs on it. There was an IBM computer. At this time I hated IBMs. I was a Macintosh guy. He said, "Let me show you something." Then he hit some buttons. About two and a half minutes later my exact track record came out for my silver system.

This track record had taken me lots of time and lots of money, because I had to find somebody who could program, somebody who had a computer, and somebody who had the data. In short, I had to hire three different people to write it for me.

Within minutes this guy had my entire silver system appear on a desk top by pushing a few buttons. I was impressed. It cost $3,000. The name of the system was SystemWriter.

I grabbed everybody I knew, and I knew everybody, and I said, "Come over here. You've got to buy this!"

They said, "What is it?"

I said, "Just give this guy $3,000 and take one home. You're going to like it."

FIGURE 1 - OMEGA TRADESTATION CHART (HIHO SILVER)

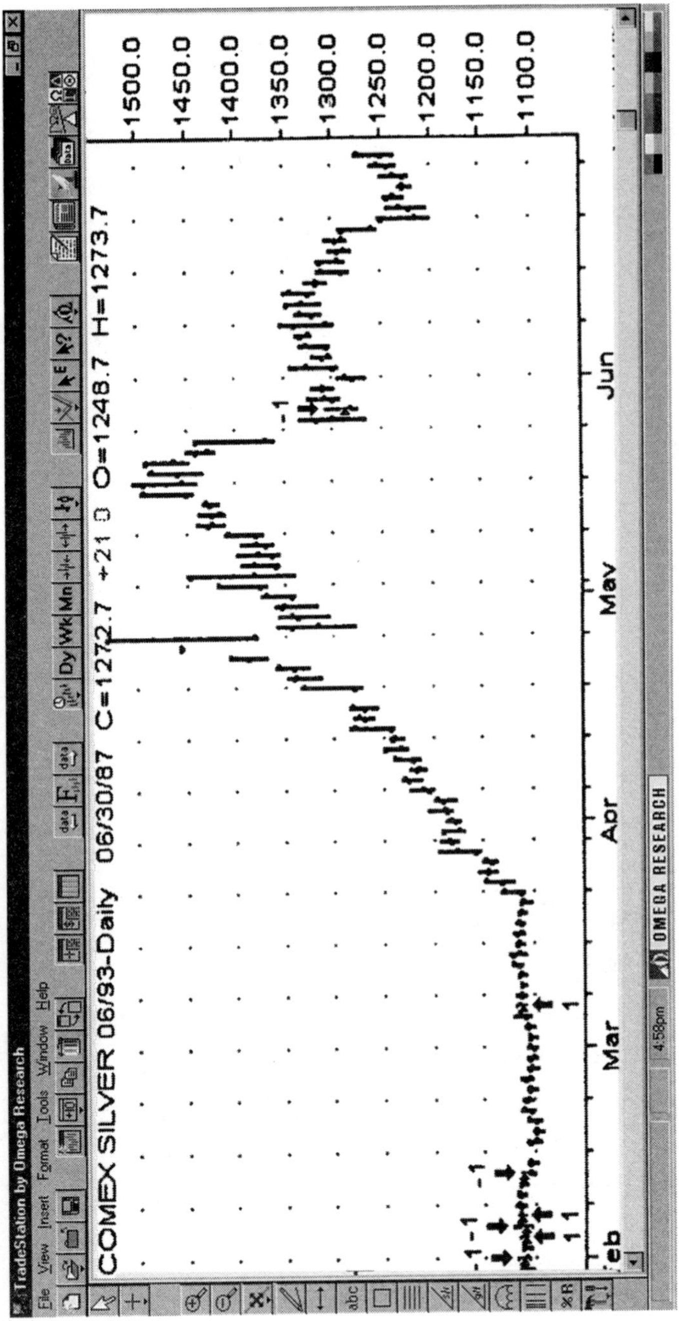

FIGURE 2
OMEGA TRADESTATION (HIHO SILVER)

```
//////////////////////////////////////////////\\\\\\\\\\\\\\\\\\\\\\\\\\\\\\\\\\\\\\\\\
                        SYSTEM

Name       : HiHo Silver
Notes : Joe Krutsinger's 1982 Silver System

Last Update : 09/11/93 06:44pm
Printed on  : 09/11/93 08:32pm
Verified    : YES

/////////////////////////////////////////// CODE \\\\\\\\\\\\\\\\\\\\\\\\\\\\\\\\\\\\\\\\\

If C > @Average(C,32) then buy tomorrow at market;
  If C < @Average(C,32) then sell tomorrow at market;



//////////////////////////////////////////////\\\\\\\\\\\\\\\\\\\\\\\\\\\\\\\\\\\\\\\\\

Prepared using Omega TradeStation Version 3.01 by Omega Research, Inc.
```

FIGURE 3
HIHO SILVER FROM COMMODITY COOKBOOK

HiHo Silver COMEX SILVER 06/93-Daily 07/29/71 - 06/30/93

**Performance Summary: All Trades**

| | | | |
|---|---|---|---|
| Total net profit | $ 243480.00 | Open position P/L | $ 310.00 |
| Gross profit | $ 502125.00 | Gross loss | $-258645.00 |
| Total # of trades | 489 | Percent profitable | 24% |
| Number winning trades | 117 | Number losing trades | 372 |
| Largest winning trade | $ 107845.00 | Largest losing trade | $ -7530.00 |
| Average winning trade | $ 4291.67 | Average losing trade | $ -695.28 |
| Ratio avg win/avg loss | 6.17 | Avg trade(win & loss) | $ 497.91 |
| Max consec. winners | 3 | Max consec. losers | 29 |
| Avg # bars in winners | 29 | Avg # bars in losers | 6 |
| Max intraday drawdown | $ -56945.00 | | |
| Profit factor | 1.94 | Max # contracts held | 1 |
| Account size required | $ 59945.00 | Return on account | 406% |

**Performance Summary: Long Trades**

| | | | |
|---|---|---|---|
| Total net profit | $ 91405.00 | Open position P/L | $ 310.00 |
| Gross profit | $ 223325.00 | Gross loss | $-131920.00 |
| Total # of trades | 244 | Percent profitable | 23% |
| Number winning trades | 56 | Number losing trades | 188 |
| Largest winning trade | $ 82595.00 | Largest losing trade | $ -5705.00 |
| Average winning trade | $ 3987.95 | Average losing trade | $ -701.70 |
| Ratio avg win/avg loss | 5.68 | Avg trade(win & loss) | $ 374.61 |
| Max consec. winners | 6 | Max consec. losers | 27 |
| Avg # bars in winners | 26 | Avg # bars in losers | 5 |
| Max intraday drawdown | $ -62015.00 | | |
| Profit factor | 1.69 | Max # contracts held | 1 |
| Account size required | $ 65015.00 | Return on account | 141% |

**Performance Summary: Short Trades**

| | | | |
|---|---|---|---|
| Total net profit | $ 152075.00 | Open position P/L | $ 0.00 |
| Gross profit | $ 278800.00 | Gross loss | $-126725.00 |
| Total # of trades | 245 | Percent profitable | 25% |
| Number winning trades | 61 | Number losing trades | 184 |
| Largest winning trade | $ 107845.00 | Largest losing trade | $ -7530.00 |
| Average winning trade | $ 4570.49 | Average losing trade | $ -688.72 |
| Ratio avg win/avg loss | 6.64 | Avg trade(win & loss) | $ 620.71 |
| Max consec. winners | 4 | Max consec. losers | 16 |
| Avg # bars in winners | 32 | Avg # bars in losers | 6 |
| Max intraday drawdown | $ -35915.00 | | |
| Profit factor | 2.20 | Max # contracts held | 1 |
| Account size required | $ 38915.00 | Return on account | 391% |

Bill sold seven of them that day; these were his first retail sales. Since he enjoyed meeting me, he gave me one free. I took it home, and I was appalled. First of all, I had to buy a new IBM computer because I did not have one.

After I hooked it up, I discovered that the manual was just a few Xeroxed pages. I pushed some buttons, and the screen said, "This test is going to take four and a half days." Four and a half days! I wondered what I had done wrong, but I did not know how to shut it down. I could not call Bill Cruz and ask him what had happened, because he thought I was a smart guy.

Bill was a lot less busy then than he is now. He called me three times a day and said, "Have you had a chance to look at it?" I kept saying, "I'm too busy to look at it now." Actually, I had let it run, and the thing was still running!

Much later I learned what I had done wrong. There were 50 indicators, and I had accidentally instructed the machine to consider all 50 indicators in every possible combination when I chose one-year British Pound data and put it on alternate.

Believe it or not, at the end of four and a half days, of the top 50 systems, all of them had a single component. Mathematically, how likely is that?

I am going to teach you this component at the end of this chapter. It has been at the base of most of my trading systems since that day, and I think it will be at the base of most of yours. Let's look and see if this component is any good. (See Figure 4 and 5.)

FIGURE 4
PAUL REVERE'S BRITISH POUND SYSTEM

```
///////////////////////////////////////////\\\\\\\\\\\\\\\\\\\\\\\\\\\\\\\\\\\\\\\\\\\\\\
Directory : C:\MAY                                Printed on    : 06/10/93 12:05pm

                              PERFORMANCE SUMMARY

Model Name          : Joe's Paul Revere           Developer      : Krutsinger
Test Number         :        1 of      1
Notes : 1000 mm stop

Data                : BRITISH POUND       12/92
Calc Dates          : 03/03/75 - 12/31/92

 Num. Conv. P. Value  Comm  Slippage  Margin  Format  Drive:\Path\FileName
--------------------------------------------------------------------------------
   26    2  $   6.250  $ 50   $  0   $  3,000  Omega   C:\20DATA\F008.DTA

//////////////////////////////// ALL TRADES  - Test 1 \\\\\\\\\\\\\\\\\\\\\\\\\\\\\\\\

Total net profit          $221,987.50
Gross profit              $461,762.50   Gross loss                 -239,775.00

Total # of trades              423      Percent profitable              38%
Number winning trades          163      Number losing trades            260

Largest winning trade      $14,712.50   Largest losing trade       $-2,387.50
Average winning trade      $2,832.90    Average losing trade       $ -922.21
Ratio avg win/avg loss          3.07    Avg trade (win & loss)        $524.79

Max consecutive winners          6      Max consecutive losers            7
Avg # bars in winners           13      Avg # bars in losers              4

Max closed-out drawdown  $-12,875.00    Max intra-day drawdown    $-13,025.00
Profit factor                   1.92    Max # of contracts held           1
Account size required     $16,025.00    Return on account             1,385%

                          Highlights - All trades
     Description                          Date        Time        Amount
     -------------------------------------------------------------------
     Largest Winning Trade                08/30/90     -    $    14,712.50
     Largest Losing Trade                 09/24/90     -    $    -2,387.50
     Largest String of + Trades           09/16/85     -                 6
     Largest String of - Trades           09/23/82     -                 7
     Maximum Closed-Out Drawdown          08/07/92     -    $   -12,875.00
     Maximum Intra-Day Drawdown           08/14/92     -    $   -13,025.00

//////////////////////////////// LONG TRADES  - Test 1 \\\\\\\\\\\\\\\\\\\\\\\\\\\\\\\

Total net profit          $108,825.00
Gross profit              $231,437.50   Gross loss                 -122,612.50

Total # of trades              213      Percent profitable              39%
Number winning trades           84      Number losing trades            129

Largest winning trade      $14,712.50   Largest losing trade       $-2,300.00
Average winning trade      $2,755.21    Average losing trade       $ -950.48
Ratio avg win/avg loss          2.89    Avg trade (win & loss)        $510.92

Max consecutive winners          7      Max consecutive losers •         10
Avg # bars in winners           19      Avg # bars in losers              3
```

# MY PAUL REVERE BRITISH POUND SYSTEM

Figure 4 on page 7 shows the trading system from March 3, 1975 through December 31, 1992. It is figured with $50 commissions and $3,000 margins, and it is trading one contract of British Pound. This is a hypothetical, simulated 18-year track record.

It made $221,987.50. It did 423 trades, which is certainly a significant occurrence. Thirty-eight percent of the trades are correct. The largest winning trade is $14,712.50. The largest losing trade is $2,387.50. There are six winners in a row and seven losers in a row.

It holds winners 19 days on average. It holds losers four days on average. The biggest drawdown was $12,875.00 over the history of the contract.

Divide $12,875.00 into $221,987.50. The drawdown to equity ratio is about 17 to 1. A good system will be 10 to 1. In my opinion, this is a great trading system.

## The Daddy-Go-to-Town Number

I have three daughters. They are all smart. I tried to teach them all I could about commodities. When one of my daughters was about six years old, she could understand everything on the SystemWriter sheet except one number. She could not understand the number for average trade.

She said, "Daddy, I understand what an average winning trade is, because that's the winners divided by this number. I understand what the average losing trade is, because that's the

FIGURE 5
PAUL REVERE'S BRITISH POUND SYSTEM

| | | | |
|---|---|---|---|
| Max closed-out drawdown | $-17,431.25 | Max intra-day drawdown | $-17,681.25 |
| Profit factor | 1.88 | Max # of contracts held | 1 |
| Account size required | $20,681.25 | Return on account | 526% |

Highlights - Long trades

| Description | Date | Time | Amount |
|---|---|---|---|
| Largest Winning Trade | 08/30/90 | - | $ 14,712.50 |
| Largest Losing Trade | 04/22/75 | - | $ -2,300.00 |
| Largest String of + Trades | 02/03/78 | - | 7 |
| Largest String of - Trades | 06/26/89 | - | 10 |
| Maximum Closed-Out Drawdown | 02/28/85 | - | $ -17,431.25 |
| Maximum Intra-Day Drawdown | 03/14/85 | - | $ -17,681.25 |

////////////////////////////// SHORT TRADES - Test 1 \\\\\\\\\\\\\\\\\\\\\\\\\\\\\\

| | | | |
|---|---|---|---|
| Total net profit | $113,162.50 | | |
| Gross profit | $230,325.00 | Gross loss | -117,162.50 |
| Total # of trades | 210 | Percent profitable | 37% |
| Number winning trades | 79 | Number losing trades | 131 |
| Largest winning trade | $13,212.50 | Largest losing trade | $-2,387.50 |
| Average winning trade | $2,915.51 | Average losing trade | $ -894.37 |
| Ratio avg win/avg loss | 3.25 | Avg trade (win & loss) | $538.87 |
| Max consecutive winners | 5 | Max consecutive losers | 10 |
| Avg # bars in winners | 18 | Avg # bars in losers | 4 |
| Max closed-out drawdown | $-18,162.50 | Max intra-day drawdown | $-18,350.00 |
| Profit factor | 1.96 | Max # of contracts held | 1 |
| Account size required | $21,350.00 | Return on account | 530% |

Highlights - Short trades

| Description | Date | Time | Amount |
|---|---|---|---|
| Largest Winning Trade | 09/29/92 | - | $ 13,212.50 |
| Largest Losing Trade | 09/24/90 | - | $ -2,387.50 |
| Largest String of + Trades | 02/27/85 | - | 5 |
| Largest String of - Trades | 08/22/79 | - | 10 |
| Maximum Closed-Out Drawdown | 09/08/92 | - | $ -18,162.50 |
| Maximum Intra-Day Drawdown | 09/10/92 | - | $ -18,350.00 |

\\\\\\\\\\\\\\\\\\\\\\\\\\\\\\\\\\\\\\\\\\\\\\//////////////////////////////////////////////

Prepared using System Writer Plus Version 2.18 by Omega Research, Inc.

losers divided by that number, but I don't understand what that average trade number is."

I said, "Honey, that's the Daddy-go-to-town number."

She said, "What do you mean?"

I said, "Well, Daddy went to town 423 times since 1975, and every time Daddy went to town he came home with $524.79 in his pocket. Your decision, when you are trying to pick a trading system, is—should you send Daddy to town or not?"

She looked at me and said, "Daddy, go to town!"

What it all boils down to is this: What is the average trade? Is it over $150? Can it stand some slippage and commission? Is the ratio between total net profits and drawdown better than 10 to 1? This one is far better. It is a terrific trading system.

I will give you the rules. They are very difficult. The buy rule is: Buy tomorrow at the highest high of the last six days on a stop. The sell rule is: Sell tomorrow at the lowest low of the last six days on a stop. Use a $1,000 money management stop after day of entry.

Let me tell you why Paul Revere is such a powerful system. First of all, let's look at moving average systems. Those of us who have traded often have bought moving average crossovers where the close went above the crossover, and now we are long.

## A Market That Tanks

Pretend you are trading soybeans or corn. All of a sudden the market tanks like that seen in Figure 6.

The moving average is like this: We are long here. We got stopped out here, and we lose this piece of money.

FIGURE 6 - A MARKET THAT TANKS

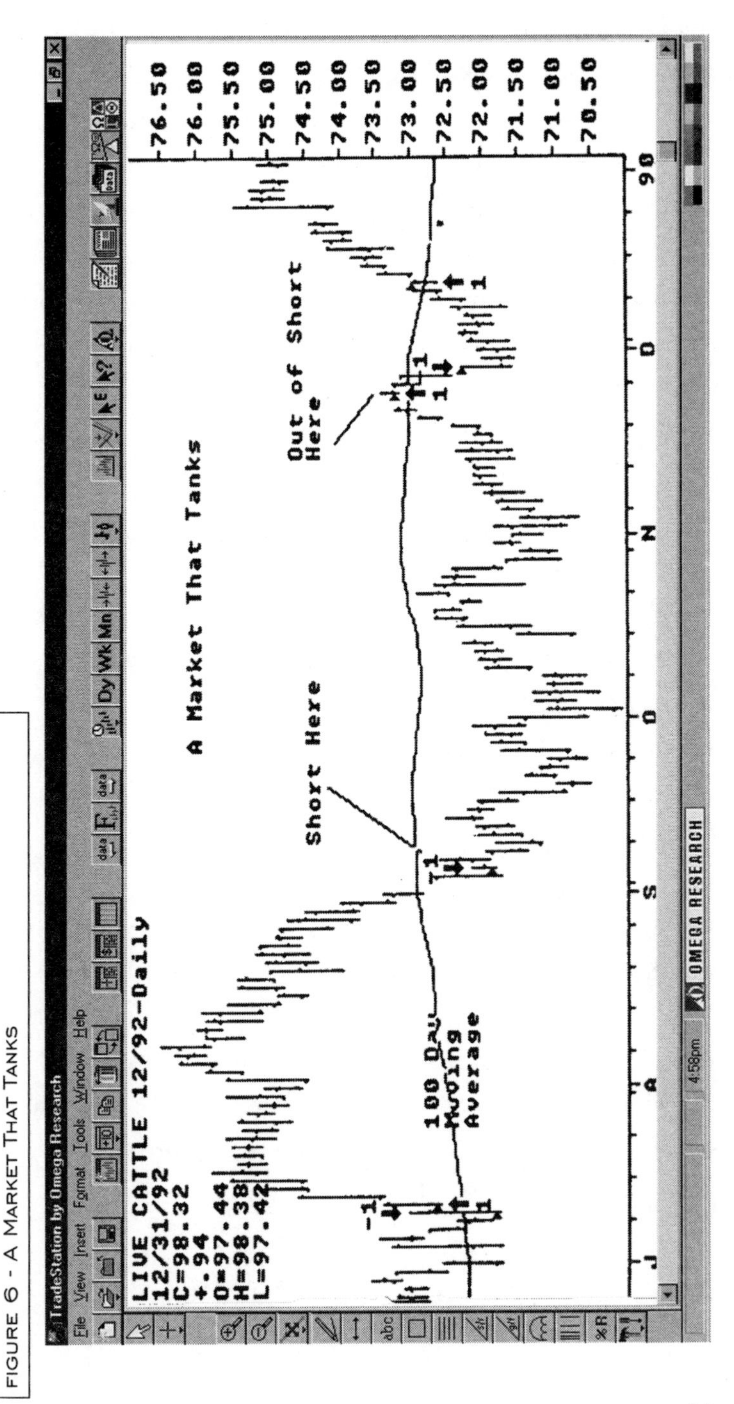

## A Channel Breakout System

A channel breakout system will be a little different. It isbuy at the highest high of the last six. Then it hase a stop at the lowest low of the last six. Then it reverses.

In a dynamic market where it runs away from indicators, a channel system is vastly superior.

## A Choppy Market

What about something that happens quite often–a choppy market? (See Figure 7.)

Indicators go flat in a choppy market, so you buy it here, sell it here, buy it here, and you sell it here. You chop up, pay commissions and slippage. Finally, hopefully, it breaks out and you make some money.

## Channel System

With a channel system–highest high, lowest low–you aren't going to be doing anything in these choppy markets. The only time period when an indicator-based system is better than a channel-based system is similar to the one in Figure 8.

You have seen this in some of the chart books. It is like a sine curve. It is a perfect market where the indicator buys it here and sells it here. This has sold a lot of computers, by the way.

FIGURE 7 - A CHOPPY MARKET

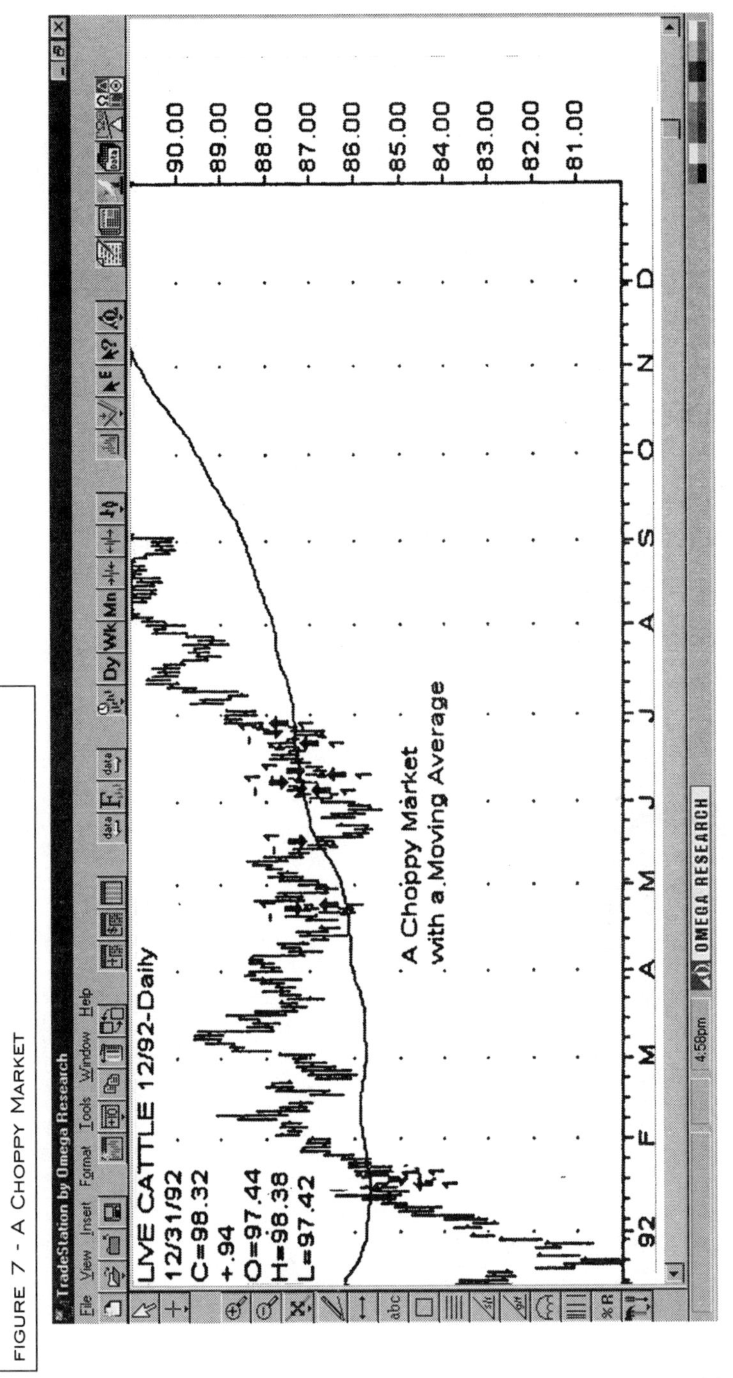

FIGURE 8 - A CHANNEL SYSTEM

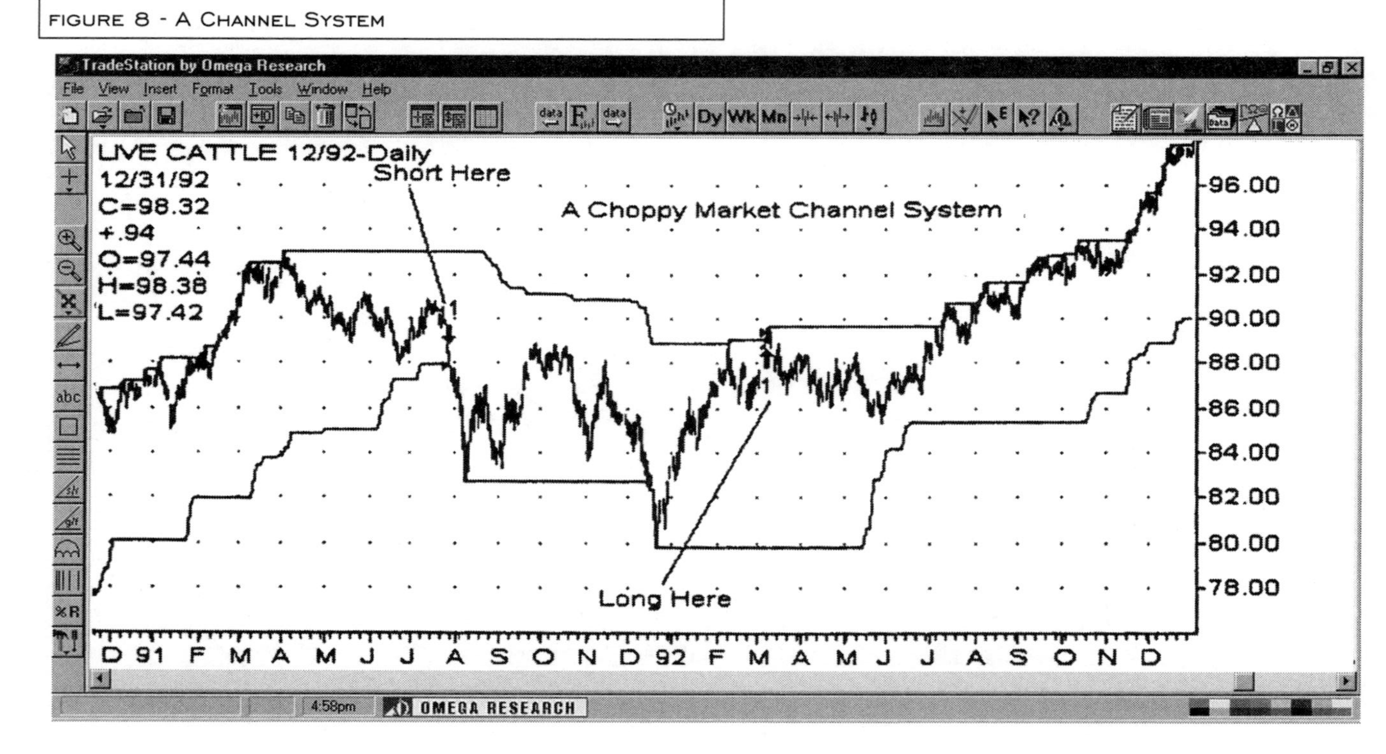

These are beautiful systems. With a channel system you always buy a little higher and sell a little lower than that perfect system. Do you notice in all three types of markets the channel system makes a little money or stands aside? It is an interesting system.

What I am suggesting you do is take this idea and steal it from me to add to your own system. Let us pretend you are going to buy when Johnny's moving average is above Jimmy's moving average.

Instead of buying at the market, say if the 10-day moving average is above the 20 or whatever it is, then buy tomorrow at the highest high of the last two on the stop. That means the market will have to go in your direction to get you in. You combine the idea of the channel (which is a great stand-alone British Pound system) into your own work.

## EXITING WITH A LOSS

You can exit MOC (market on close). You can exit with a money management stop of $1,000, or you can exit with the lowest low or highest high of a couple of days. You can also exit so many bars since entry.

If you have a 20-day moving average and you are 12 days into the trade, don't you think that it is probably going to lose momentum coming into the next little cycle of the moving average? It does.

Here is one way to test a system like that. If you have a 20-day moving average, tell your system to arbitrarily get out after 11 days. Let's say your 20-day moving average gets you in right here (see Figure 9).

Count out until you get to 11. Eleven days will take you out over here, probably even before the crossover does. By arbitrarily getting out at 11 days it not only resets your system, but makes your system put you in a new system if it should happen.

## EXITING WITH A PROFIT

Possible exit with profit techniques: Exit market on close, exit after six bars in trade, exit with a profit objective (arbitrarily pick $1,000), or exit at resistance or support levels. If long, exit at the highest high of the last six days. If short, exit at the lowest low of the last six days.

## REVIEW

In review, I have taken a very old system that Richard Donchian developed in 1962 called Channel Breakout and shown you a number of ways to incorporate it into your own systems.

Look at the British Pound system. It is a traditional market that everybody trades with moving averages, because they say it is trending. You can trade this British Pound system without a computer, because all you need to know is the high and the low every day. Record them on an Excel spreadsheet, and pick out the highest value and the lowest value. If the price today closes above the highest high of the last six, you are long. If it closes below the lowest low of the last six, you are short.

The next thing I ask you to do is take the channel system and incorporate it into your own trading system. Think of the

FIGURE 9 - EXIT AFTER 11 DAYS

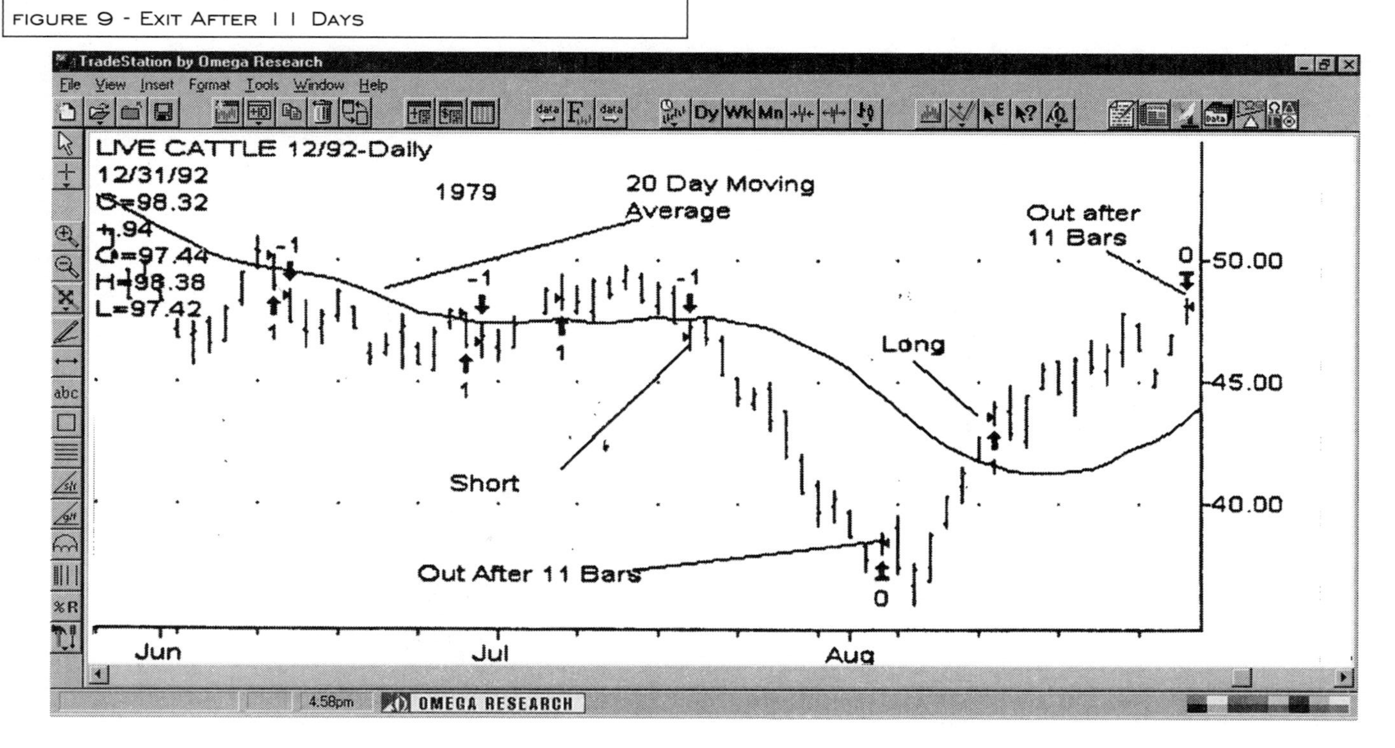

dynamics of this. You decide your own way of getting in, but it makes the train go your way.

Let me explain this. If you are in Chicago wanting to travel to New York, isn't it a lot smarter to get on a train that is heading east than to get on a train that is heading west, hoping it will turn around? But everybody trades commodities getting on a westbound train, hoping it will go to New York. Adding this concept to your own system should help you do very well.

## TAILORING A SYSTEM FOR YOURSELF

We are going to talk about tailoring a system to fit your temperament and personality. The three critical components are market entry (getting in with our chosen indicator), exiting with a profit, and exiting with a loss.

Remember how to evaluate a trading system? Maximum profits divided by net profit is a good rule to determine whether or not to go on. Some people say that it doesn't matter if a system is right 25 percent of the time or 80 percent of the time. It is the bottom line that counts.

They are lying to you. Anybody who gets a confirm day after day that shows loser after loser will eventually say, "This isn't for me." People who get winner after winner after winner statements, then all of a sudden get a statement with a very large loss on it, will also become disenchanted.

I am going to emphasize bet size a little bit more. Bet size is a gambling term. Some people would say it is not appropriate, but maybe it is. Commodity trading should be considered a game of chance.

This is a trading system called Joe's Paul Revere (Figure 10).

FIGURE 10
JOE'S PAUL REVERE

PAUL REVERE 03/03/75 to 12/31/92 C:\PA\
PRB(1) 2700

| | | | |
|---|---|---|---|
| Total net profit | 221,987.50 | < 241,987.50> | |
| Gross profit | 461,762.50 | Gross loss | -239,775.00 |
| Total # of trades | 423 | Percent profitable | 39% |
| Number winning trades | 163 | Number losing trades | 260 |
| Largest winning trade | 14,712.50 | Largest losing trade | -2,387.50 |
| Average winning trade | 2,832.90 | Average losing trade | -922.21 |
| Ratio avg win/avg loss | 3.07 | Avg trade (win & loss) | 524.79 |
| Max consecutive winners | 6 | Max consecutive losers | 7 |
| Avg # bars in winners | 20 | Avg # bars in losers | 5 |
| Max drawdown | 13,025.00 | Avg # of contracts held | 1 |
| Profit factor | 1.18 | Max # of contracts held | 1 |
| Account size required | 15,725.00 | Return on account | 1412% |

This is a track record from March 3, 1975 to December 31, 1992. The value of the British Pound is $6.25 a point. We have used a $50 commission, no slippage, and a $3,000 margin. It was tested using Omega continuous data. It made $221,000 plus. It had 423 trades, 39 percent which were profitable. The average winning trade is $2,832.90. The average losing trade is $922. The average winning trade or the Daddy-go-to-town number is $524. The bigger that number, the better. The more trade instances over 30, the better.

## Keep It Simple

The simpler the rules, the better. Now, remember, everything I am telling you is my opinion–the way I have developed systems. I have written about 520 systems for people all over the world. This does not mean I am the best, but I am probably one of the quickest.

I hope that you take the work I give you and make it much better, make it your own. This is my goal for giving you these rules. Remember, when I say something is better or worse, it is my opinion. If you believe something else, that is fine.

## Bet Size and Evaluating Your System

Let's talk about bet size, whether you win or lose. Pretend we are in Las Vegas. I know most of you have never gone to Las Vegas, but in Las Vegas there is a game called roulette. Half the numbers are black, and half are red. There is a 0 and a double 0, but we will pretend they are commission and ignore them.

To play roulette you put money on the table and bet black. If it comes up black, they give you back your dollar and another dollar besides. If it comes up red, they take your dollar away, and hope that you have more money in your pocket.

If a roulette wheel is perfectly balanced with no 0s or double 0s, you should win 50 percent of the time and lose 50 percent of the time. The house wins because the roulette wheel does have a 0 and double 0, and you don't stay around after you have a string of losses. This is called gambling. The bet size in this case is $1. The win or the loss in this case is $1.

### Another Way to Evaluate Your System

Look at Paul Revere as a gambling deal. Pretend we have a crooked wheel because this system is only right 38 percent of the time. That means that 62 percent of the time they are going to take your money. They are going to take $922 when you lose.

To make it easy, pretend that when you lose, you lose 92 cents, but when you win you are going to win $2.80. This means that the ratio of win to loss is 3.07 to 1. For every dollar you lose in this game, you are going to win $3. Would you play this game? Of course you would. This is another way to evaluate a trading system.

## IT IS A GAME OF CHANCE

Pretend it is a game of chance. Forget it is a commodity. Forget it has any economic value at all. It is a game of chance, and you evaluate it using the percentage of times you win, the amount of money they give you if you win, and the amount of money they take away if you lose.

## Paul Revere—the Trading Rules

We will now reiterate the trading rules of this system, so you understand. The trading rules are: Buy at the highest high of the last six days on a stop, and sell at the lowest low of the last six days on a stop. There is a $1,000 risk management stop in case someone shoots at somebody and you want to get out. These rules are all there is to this system.

## Paul Revere—Balance

Let's talk about balance. The long side of this system made $108,000, had 213 trades, and it was correct 39 percent of the time over this l-year period. If you took only the long side, the average trade size or Daddy-go-to-town number is $510.

Here is what the short side of that system looks like: Hypothetically, it made $113,162.50 with 210 trades. It was correct 37 percent of the time, and the Daddy-go-to-town number was 538.87. If you make $108,000 on the longs and $113,000 on the shorts, and you have 213 trades on the longs and 210 trades on the shorts, this is what is called balance.

## Hedging Currencies

Who would only trade the long side of a currency market? How about a bank? It would have to be someone who actually has a currency risk. This is how you could hedge currencies.

First, you would find a good system. When the system gave you a good buy signal and you needed to be long in your futures position, you would take the buy signal. When it gave you a sell signal you would liquidate. By doing this you would develop hedging programs for yourselves out of your own trading systems.

### Paul Revere—Summation

Paul Revere should hold up because it has a long history, it is not a complicated system, and the rules are very easy. Here is how you would write it in computer language: Buy tomorrow at the highest high of the last six periods on a stop, and sell tomorrow on the lowest low of the last six periods on a stop. You can trade this as a system by itself or add it to your current currency system.

## An Overview of Four Software Systems

I think it is important to see some of the tools that are available in the industry, and to see how you might want to use them to develop your system. All of the companies discussed below have either demonstration disks or something else so you can get a better hands-on feel for the software. If you did not know some of these products exist, I hope I will enlighten you.

# TRADESTATION

TradeStation is used after you discover your Holy Grail. When you want to be able to implement your new system you type it onto TradeStation. Then when it beeps, you do what it says.

One of the reasons I went with Robbins Trading was to help them train a staff who would implement the systems. Clients had systems, but they were not trading them, so I helped develop a staff who could read the software, listen to it beep, and put in the order.

What do you suppose happened? They put in the trades. They did not wait to see how it was going to open or think, "It's Tuesday. I don't want to do it because there may be a cattle report." They just followed the systems, listened to the beeps, and implemented the trades.

Implementation is the key to commodity trading. No matter what your system is, make your plan. Then follow your plan. It is very simple.

# SYSTEMWRITER

SystemWriter is a system development tool. It can be used when you come up with an idea, and you want to see the best moving average, the best indicator, and the best stop. Use it when you want to really dig into research, and come up with what you think is your Holy Grail.

## ONE DAY AT A TIME

One Day at a Time is more of a teaching tool that will let you look at old data and ask, "What would I have done in this situation?" You can then move it up one day at a time until you see what it actually did.

It is a great teaching tool not only for technical traders, but for people who want to look at the fundamentals of a market. They remember back to 1987. They remember back to 1975. They can pull up the data, show that piece of data, and see what they would have done.

## PORTANA

Portana is a wonderful product that will allow you to take your research from SystemWriter, lay it together, and see what happens if you do all these things at once using real money. It shows you what has happened historically.

### Tools Do Not Make the Builder

Let me tell you about tools. My father was a master mechanic. People would bring their cars on flatbed trucks from hundreds of miles around to my dad's house. He would take the car off the truck, drive it around, and tell them how to fix it. This was before Sun Technologies would let you analyze what was wrong with a car.

Dad could get a hammer at K-Mart and build a car. I could get a set of S & K tools and still not be able to change a tire. Tools do not make the builder, but it is much easier to loosen a screw with a screwdriver than it is with a hammer. You can do them both, but it is easier on the screw and the person if you have the right tool.

I would suggest, if you're going to invest the time and the effort in commodity trading, to get some tools even if they are lower level ones. My dad, as good a mechanic as he was, would not have taken nuts off with his bare hands. He used the lug wrench. I suggest you use some of these products that are available.

Look at One Night Stand Trading System. You are supposed to buy at the highest high of so many days on a Friday. You will not do it, because the market is making a new high on a Friday. This high is higher than it has been for eight days, so you decide to wait and try to buy it cheaper.

Psychologically, you do not want to carry it over the weekend. You will watch this trade, and you will watch it and you will watch it. In the last five years you would have watched it 463 times. It is very difficult to implement your own system.

# The Software Tools You May Need

## TRADESTATION

The first product we are going to discuss is TradeStation. It is the most complicated of the four software systems, the most sophisticated, and the most expensive. The trading system we are going to use applying TradeStation is: "If today is Friday, then buy tomorrow at the market." As you can see in Figure 11, this is pretty much how the system is written.

The system is called Buy Monday, and the system is written, "If day of week is 5 (in other words, if today is Friday), then buy tomorrow at the market." This is done in the section of TradeStation marked Quick Editor.

Most software programs on the market today have no Quick Editor. They are simply charting packages that let you look at a chart and decide, "Oh, I'd like to buy it here, and I'd like to sell it here."

Both SystemWriter and TradeStation will let you write your strategy, test it on the data, and see what hypothetically would have or could have happened. We are going to go into the analysis section of TradeStation to turn on that system we wrote called Buy Monday. We will check our stops, and then we will say, "The first test we will do is with no stops at all, but we will close all trades at end of day."

For costs, I've put down $55 commissions and a $3,000 margin, although we are trading it intraday, so there really is no margin consideration except for whatever your firm charges for a daytrade. (Refer to Figure 11.)

FIGURE 11 - BUY MONDAY

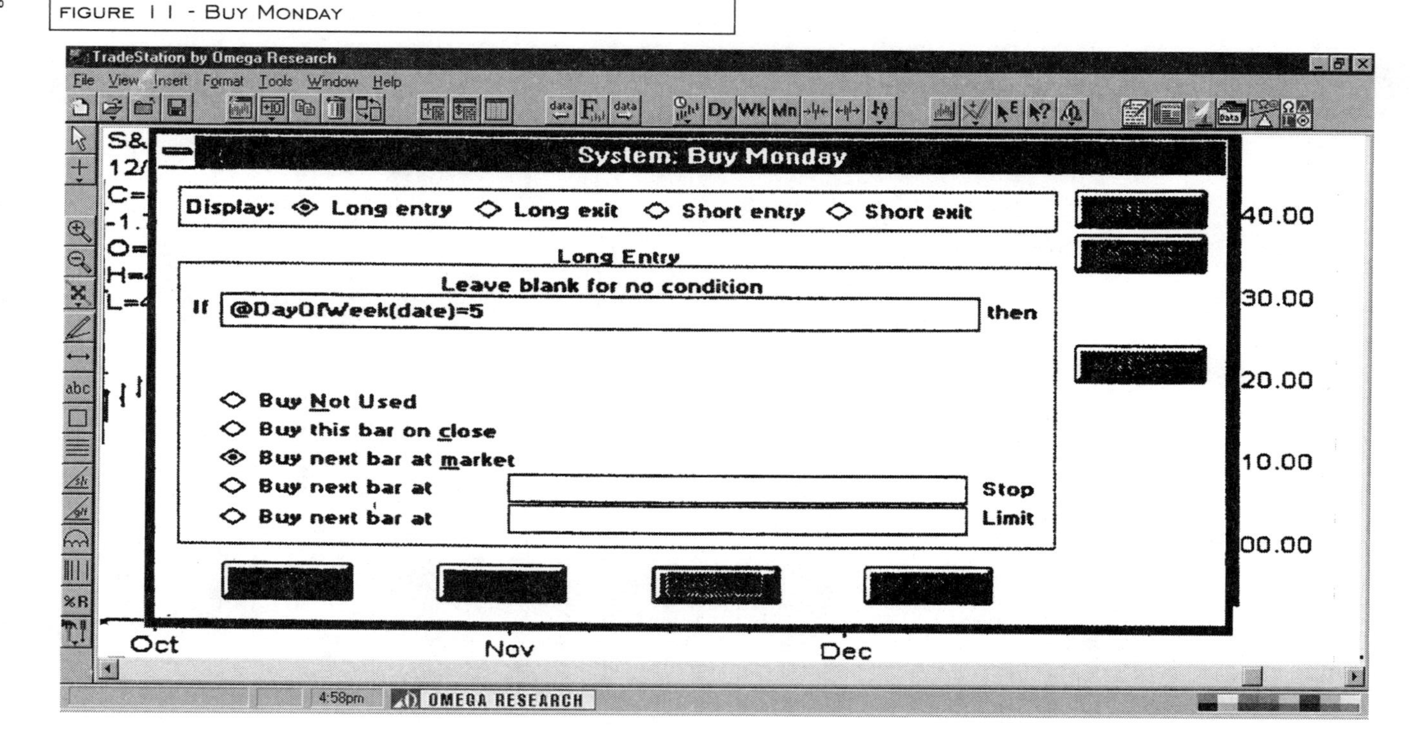

FIGURE 12 - CHART FOR BUY MONDAY

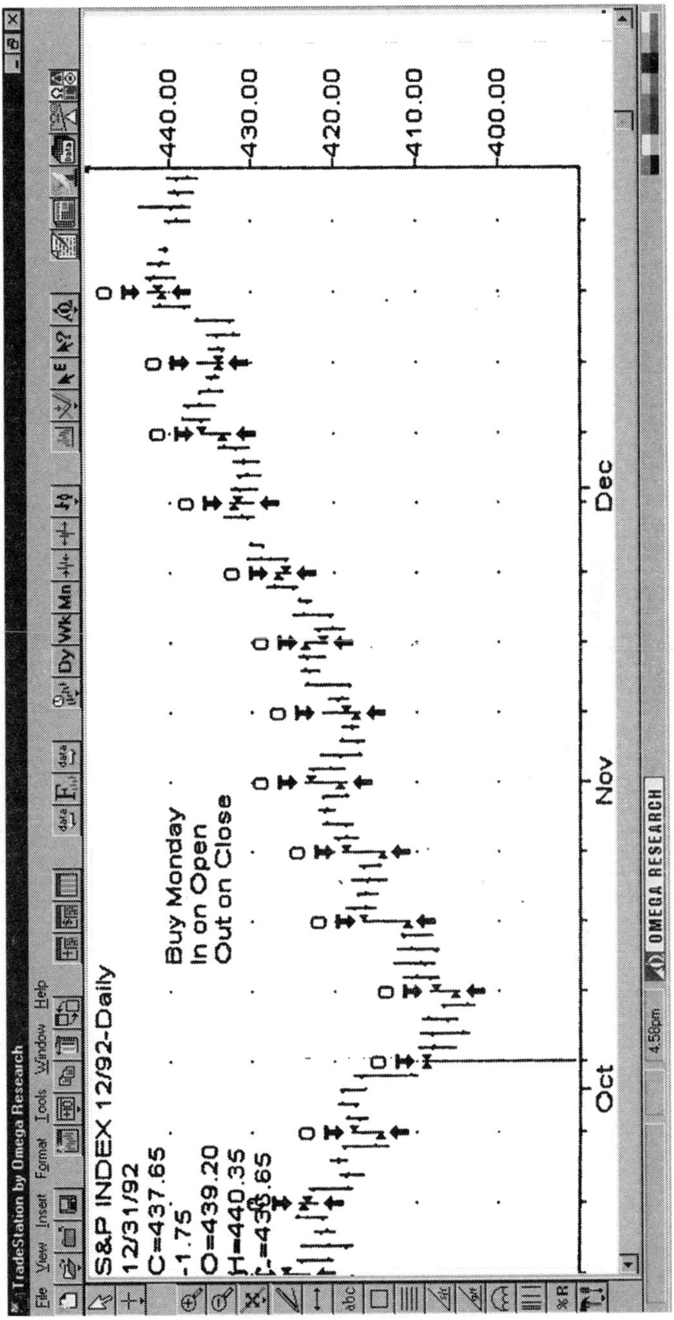

Figure 12 shows a test over daily bars historical from 1988 through 1992. It covers five years of every day of the S&P 500 futures.

See all this activity? Since it is a buy only system, it is buying only on Mondays, and then getting out on the close. It tells you where you got in with the green arrows and the green flags. It tells you where you got out with the white squat bars. White squat bars with a zero means that you are flat. Green means that you are in the market.

## Using TradeStation

I am going to tell TradeStation to show me a performance summary very similar to what we saw for the British Pound system. How long do you think it will take it to do a 10-year study on this chart? Less than one second (see Figures 13 and 14).

TradeStation is a very smart program. Whenever I pull up a chart, it will automatically figure the next step that is normally taken.

It is showing me longs only. It made approximately $77,000, had 251 trades, and was 56% right. The average winner is $1,270. The average loser is $906. The average trade is $307. The drawdown is approximately $13,000 over this period. This is testing from January 4, 1988 to December 31, 1992, five years of doing nothing but buying on Mondays and getting out on the close with no stops. I think it is a pretty interesting program.

If you divide the $13,000 drawdown into the $77,000 net profit, you get a six to one ratio. This is not as good as some of

FIGURE 13
PERFORMANCE SUMMARY OF BUY MONDAY

```
Buy Monday  S&P INDEX 12/92-Daily    01/04/88 - 12/31/92

                          Performance Summary:  All Trades

Total net profit          $  77225.00   Open position P/L         $       0.00
Gross profit              $ 177800.00   Gross loss                $-100575.00

Total # of trades                251    Percent profitable             56%
Number winning trades            140    Number losing trades          111

Largest winning trade     $  10275.00   Largest losing trade      $  -5350.00
Average winning trade     $   1270.00   Average losing trade      $   -906.08
Ratio avg win/avg loss           1.40   Avg trade(win & loss)     $    307.67

Max consec. winners               11    Max consec. losers               7
Avg # bars in winners              0    Avg # bars in losers             0

Max intraday drawdown     $ -13200.00
Profit factor                    1.77   Max # contracts held             1
Account size required     $  16200.00   Return on account              477%
-- - - -- - - -- - - -- - - -- - - -- - - -- - - -- - - -- - - -- - - -- - -

                          Performance Summary:  Long Trades

Total net profit          $  77225.00   Open position P/L         $       0.00
Gross profit              $ 177800.00   Gross loss                $-100575.00

Total # of trades                251    Percent profitable             56%
Number winning trades            140    Number losing trades          111

Largest winning trade     $  10275.00   Largest losing trade      $  -5350.00
Average winning trade     $   1270.00   Average losing trade      $   -906.08
Ratio avg win/avg loss           1.40   Avg trade(win & loss)     $    307.67

Max consec. winners               11    Max consec. losers               7
Avg # bars in winners              0    Avg # bars in losers             0

Max intraday drawdown     $ -13200.00
Profit factor                    1.77   Max # contracts held             1
Account size required     $  16200.00   Return on account              477%
-- - - -- - - -- - - -- - - -- - - -- - - -- - - -- - - -- - - -- - - -- - -

                          Performance Summary:  Short Trades

Total net profit          $       0.00  Open position P/L         $       0.00
Gross profit              $       0.00  Gross loss                $       0.00

Total # of trades                  0    Percent profitable              0%
Number winning trades              0    Number losing trades             0

Largest winning trade     $       0.00  Largest losing trade      $       0.00
Average winning trade     $       0.00  Average losing trade      $       0.00
Ratio avg win/avg loss         100.00   Avg trade(win & loss)     $       0.00

Max consec. winners                0    Max consec. losers               0
Avg # bars in winners              0    Avg # bars in losers             0

Max intraday drawdown     $       0.00
Profit factor                  100.00   Max # contracts held             0
Account size required     $       0.00  Return on account                0%
```

FIGURE 14
BUY MONDAY

```
////////////////////////////////////////\\\\\\\\\\\\\\\\\\\\\\\\\\\\\\\\\\\\\\\\
Directory : F:\KK                                  Printed on    : 10/03/93 12:30pm

                                   ENTRY SIGNAL

Signal Name      : Monday                          Developer     : KRUTSINGER
Notes :

Last Update : 09/06/93 02:55pm
Long  Entry Verified : YES
Short Entry Verified : NO

////////////////////////////////// LONG ENTRY \\\\\\\\\\\\\\\\\\\\\\\\\\

If @DayOfWeek(0)=5 then buy tomorrow at market
with ExitOnCloseOfEntryBar=True;

////////////////////////////////// SHORT ENTRY \\\\\\\\\\\\\\\\\\\\\\\\\\\\\\

////////////////////////////// VARIABLE DESCRIPTION \\\\\\\\\\\\\\\\\\\\\\\\\\

No variables used in entry signal.

////////////////////////////// MODELS USING SIGNAL \\\\\\\\\\\\\\\\\\\\\\\\\\\\\

Model Name                    Developer              Last Update
-------------------------------------------------------------------------------
Monday Buy                    KRUTSINGER           10/03/93 12:29pm

\\\\\\\\\\\\\\\\\\\\\\\\\\\\\\\\\\\\\\\\//////////////////////////////////////

Prepared using System Writer Plus Version 2.18 by Omega Research, Inc.
```

our other systems, but remember, the less words you put into a trading system, the better system it is. This is about as simple as it can get.

Now, I'm going to make a little change in the program. I'm going to put in a $1,000 stop. (See Figure 15.)

Our largest losing trade before was $5,000. Now, theoretically, our largest losing trade should be $1,000 plus commission. The software is going through the system, doing five years of work. Seconds later, the new trades are here. (See Figure 16.)

Here is the system trade by trade, and here is the profit and loss. Buy Monday made $61,000 and had an $11,000 drawdown. That is about a five to one ratio. Now our losing trade is $1,055, and the system is right about 50 percent of the time.

If this were a gambling wheel that was right 50 percent of the time, it's a straight wheel. The average winner is $1,327. The average loser is $833, and you win half the time. Would you play this game in Las Vegas? You would have to wait in a long line first.

## The Benefit of TradeStation Software

The major benefit of TradeStation is that it will take your idea no matter how complicated, apply it to the data, and beep at you (tell you what is happening) in the future. This is a very powerful helper. You do not have to sit and stare at the screen to see what is happening. TradeStation watches for you. TradeStation is a windows product developed by Omega Research.

FIGURE 15 - STOP SETTING, SHOW HOW TO DO THIS

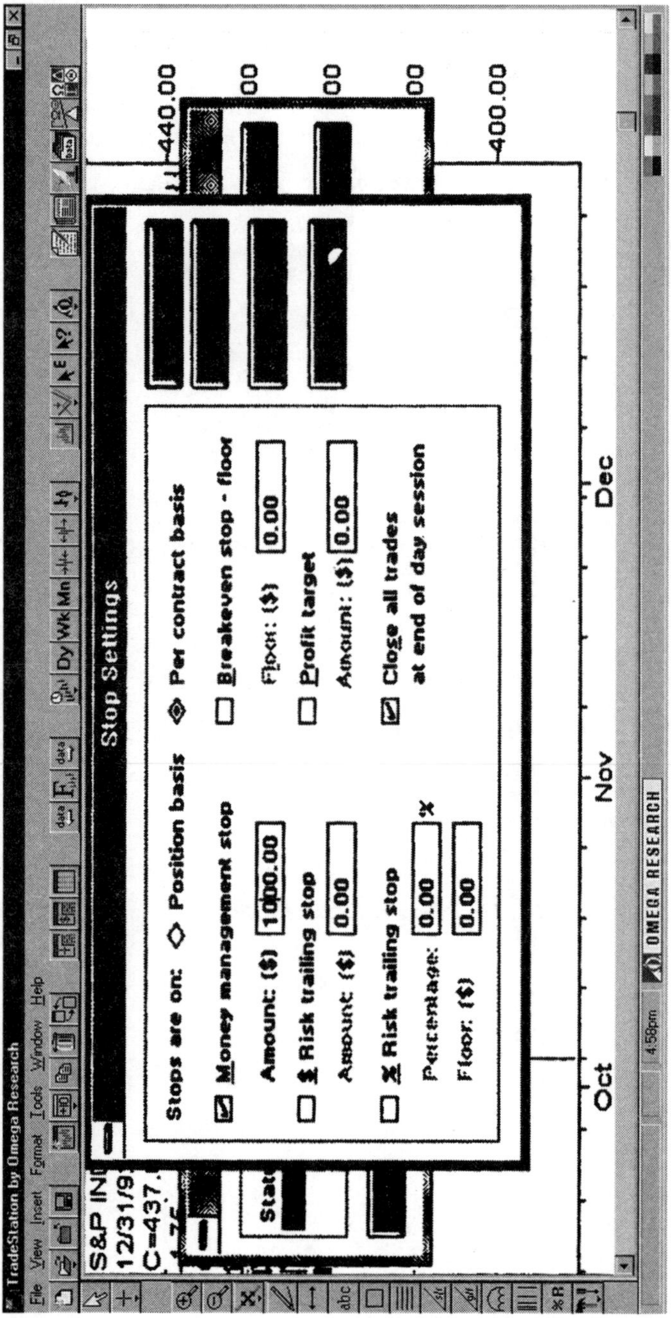

TradeStation by Omega Research
File View Insert Format Tools Window Help
Dy Wk Mn
S&P IN
12/31/9
C=437.
Stat
Stop Settings
Stops are on: Position basis Per contract basis
Money management stop
Amount: ($) 1000.00
$ Risk trailing stop
Amount: ($) 0.00
% Risk trailing stop
Percentage: 0.00 %
Floor: ($) 0.00
Breakeven stop - floor
Floor: ($) 0.00
Profit target
Amount: ($) 0.00
Close all trades
at end of day session
440.00
00
00
00
400.00
Oct
Nov
Dec
4:58pm
OMEGA RESEARCH

FIGURE 16
PERFORMANCE SUMMARY FOR BUY MONDAY

**Buy Monday S&P INDEX 12/92-Daily 01/04/88 - 12/31/92**

**Performance Summary: All Trades**

| | | | |
|---|---|---|---|
| Total net profit | $ 61485.00 | Open position P/L | $ 0.00 |
| Gross profit | $ 167295.00 | Gross loss | $-105810.00 |
| Total # of trades | 253 | Percent profitable | 50% |
| Number winning trades | 126 | Number losing trades | 127 |
| Largest winning trade | $ 10270.00 | Largest losing trade | $ -1055.00 |
| Average winning trade | $ 1327.74 | Average losing trade | $ -833.15 |
| Ratio avg win/avg loss | 1.59 | Avg trade(win & loss) | $ 243.02 |
| Max consec. winners | 11 | Max consec. losers | 7 |
| Avg # bars in winners | 0 | Avg # bars in losers | 0 |
| Max intraday drawdown | $ -11395.00 | | |
| Profit factor | 1.58 | Max # contracts held | 1 |
| Account size required | $ 14395.00 | Return on account | 427% |

**Performance Summary: Long Trades**

| | | | |
|---|---|---|---|
| Total net profit | $ 61485.00 | Open position P/L | $ 0.00 |
| Gross profit | $ 167295.00 | Gross loss | $-105810.00 |
| Total # of trades | 253 | Percent profitable | 50% |
| Number winning trades | 126 | Number losing trades | 127 |
| Largest winning trade | $ 10270.00 | Largest losing trade | $ -1055.00 |
| Average winning trade | $ 1327.74 | Average losing trade | $ -833.15 |
| Ratio avg win/avg loss | 1.59 | Avg trade(win & loss) | $ 243.02 |
| Max consec. winners | 11 | Max consec. losers | 7 |
| Avg # bars in winners | 0 | Avg # bars in losers | 0 |
| Max intraday drawdown | $ -11395.00 | | |
| Profit factor | 1.58 | Max # contracts held | 1 |
| Account size required | $ 14395.00 | Return on account | 427% |

**Performance Summary: Short Trades**

| | | | |
|---|---|---|---|
| Total net profit | $ 0.00 | Open position P/L | $ 0.00 |
| Gross profit | $ 0.00 | Gross loss | $ 0.00 |
| Total # of trades | 0 | Percent profitable | 0% |
| Number winning trades | 0 | Number losing trades | 0 |
| Largest winning trade | $ 0.00 | Largest losing trade | $ 0.00 |
| Average winning trade | $ 0.00 | Average losing trade | $ 0.00 |
| Ratio avg win/avg loss | 100.00 | Avg trade(win & loss) | $ 0.00 |
| Max consec. winners | 0 | Max consec. losers | 0 |
| Avg # bars in winners | 0 | Avg # bars in losers | 0 |
| Max intraday drawdown | $ 0.00 | | |
| Profit factor | 100.00 | Max # contracts held | 0 |
| Account size required | $ 0.00 | Return on account | 0% |

# SYSTEMWRITER

The best product I know to develop a trading system is an older product called SystemWriter. SystemWriter is a DOS product written originally in 1987 by Omega Research.

## The Benefits of SystemWriter

We can actually attach different trading ideas, different stops, different exits, on an alternate basis, and let SystemWriter find what the best stop or the best combination of systems would be in the past. This is a very powerful program. This is how I use my SystemWriter. At night before I leave my office I set up a bunch of elaborate tests, turn the machine on and the screen off, and let it run all night long. When I come back in the morning I have the results of my trading research.

I take that research and fine-tune it on my TradeStation, which is plugged into live data working on current markets. By using SystemWriter this way I can do the research of four or five different people at once.

# ONE NIGHT STAND

One Night Stand (see Figures 17 thru 22) only trades over the weekend. The Buy Monday system (S&P) only trades Mondays. So, theoretically, since the currencies open before the S&P, you never have both those positions on simultaneously.

FIGURE 17
ONE NIGHT STAND

```
//////////////////////////////////////////////////////////\\\\\\\\\\\\\\\\\\\\\\\\\\\\\\\\\\
                                    SYSTEM

Name        : One Night Stand
Notes :

Last Update : 04/27/93 09:29am
Printed on  : 06/10/93 02:14pm
Verified    : YES

//////////////////////////////////////////////////// CODE \\\\\\\\\\\\\\\\\\\\\\\\\\\\\\\\\\

If Average(C,10)[1] > Average(C,40)[1] and
 DayOfweek(date)=4 then buy tomorrow at
Highest(H,4) stop;

If Average(C,10)[1] < Average(C,40)[1] and
 DayOfweek(date)=4 then Sell tomorrow at
Lowest(L,8) stop;

If barssinceentry> 0 then exitlong at market;
If barssinceentry> 0 then exitShort at market;
If DayOfWeek(date)=5 then
ExitShort at market;
If DayOfWeek(date)=5 then
ExitLong at market;
```

FIGURE 18
ONE NIGHT STAND

```
ONE NIGHT STAND 01/04/88 to 12/31/92          C:\PA\
BP1(1)    2700  DM1(1)    2700  SF1(1)    2700  JY1(1)    2700  CL1(1)    2700
DX1(1)    2700
=========================================================================
Total net profit            115,257.50   <      135,257.50>
Gross profit                163,106.25   Gross loss                -47,848.75

Total # of trades                445     Percent profitable              65%
Number winning trades            291     Number losing trades           154

Largest winning trade         3,095.00   Largest losing trade        -2,267
Average winning trade           560.50   Average losing trade          -310
Ratio avg win/avg loss            1.80   Avg trade (win & loss)         259

Max consecutive winners           20     Max consecutive losers           9
Avg # bars in winners              1     Avg # bars in losers             1

Max drawdown                  5,700.00   Avg # of contracts held          3
Profit factor                     1.18   Max # of contracts held          6
Account size required        21,900.00   Return on account              526%
=========================================================================
```

FIGURE 19
ONE NIGHT STAND

PORTFOLIO ANALYZER YEARLY REPORT for ONE NIGHT STAND

| DATE | OPEN EQUITY | CLOSED EQUITY | TOTAL EQUITY | MAX DRAWDOWN | % DD | % CHNG TOT EQ | NUM TRADE |
|---|---|---|---|---|---|---|---|
| 880104 | 0.00 | 20000.00 | 20000.00 | 0.00 | 0.0 | 0.0 | 0 |
| 881230 | 180.00 | 33297.50 | 33477.50 | 5687.50 | 28.4 | 67.4 | 1 |
| 891229 | 0.00 | 48740.00 | 48740.00 | 5700.00 | 17.1 | 45.6 | 0 |
| 901231 | 0.00 | 77167.50 | 77167.50 | 5700.00 | 10.0 | 58.3 | 0 |
| 911231 | 0.00 | 115022.50 | 115022.50 | 5700.00 | 6.0 | 49.1 | 0 |
| 921231 | 0.00 | 135257.50 | 135257.50 | 5700.00 | 4.9 | 17.6 | [illegible] |

FIGURE 20
ONE NIGHT STAND

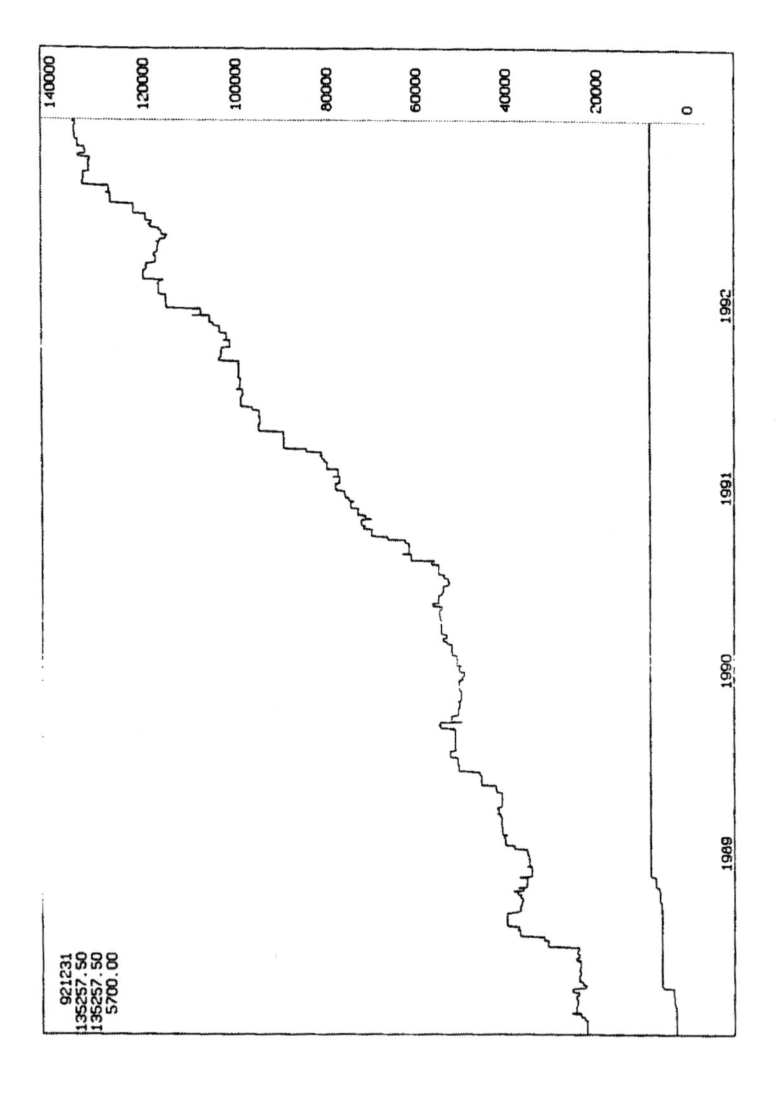

FIGURE 21
ONE NIGHT STAND

PORTFOLIO ANALYZER QUARTLY REPORT for ONE NIGHT STAND

| DATE | OPEN EQUITY | CLOSED EQUITY | TOTAL EQUITY | MAX DRAWDOWN | % DD | % CHNG TOT EQ | NUM TRADE |
|---|---|---|---|---|---|---|---|
| 880104 | 0.00 | 20000.00 | 20000.00 | 0.00 | 0.0 | 0.0 | 0 |
| 880331 | 0.00 | 23282.50 | 23282.50 | 605.00 | 3.0 | 16.4 | 0 |
| 880630 | 0.00 | 28747.50 | 28747.50 | 3153.75 | 15.8 | 23.5 | 0 |
| 880930 | 380.00 | 34390.00 | 34770.00 | 3627.50 | 18.1 | 20.9 | [illegible] |
| 881230 | 180.00 | 33297.50 | 33477.50 | 5687.50 | 28.4 | -3.7 | [illegible] |
| 890331 | -985.00 | 40142.50 | 39157.50 | 5687.50 | 28.2 | 17.0 | [illegible] |
| 890630 | 0.00 | 49230.00 | 49230.00 | 5687.50 | 19.5 | 25.7 | [illegible] |
| 890929 | -840.00 | 50507.50 | 49667.50 | 5687.50 | 17.1 | 0.9 | [illegible] |
| 891229 | 0.00 | 48740.00 | 48740.00 | 5700.00 | 17.1 | -1.9 | [illegible] |
| 900330 | 0.00 | 52860.00 | 52860.00 | 5700.00 | 17.1 | 8.5 | [illegible] |
| 900629 | 280.00 | 51240.00 | 51520.00 | 5700.00 | 16.4 | -2.5 | [illegible] |
| 900928 | 0.00 | 68965.00 | 68965.00 | 5700.00 | 11.6 | 33.9 | [illegible] |
| 901231 | 0.00 | 77167.50 | 77167.50 | 5700.00 | 10.0 | 11.9 | [illegible] |
| 910329 | 0.00 | 89007.50 | 89007.50 | 5700.00 | 8.3 | 15.3 | [illegible] |
| 910628 | -292.50 | 98500.00 | 98207.50 | 5700.00 | 7.3 | 10.3 | [illegible] |
| 910930 | 0.00 | 102575.00 | 102575.00 | 5700.00 | 6.8 | 4.4 | [illegible] |
| 911231 | 0.00 | 115022.50 | 115022.50 | 5700.00 | 6.0 | 12.1 | [illegible] |
| 920331 | 0.00 | 117295.00 | 117295.00 | 5700.00 | 5.7 | 2.0 | 0 |
| 920630 | 0.00 | 122057.50 | 122057.50 | 5700.00 | 5.6 | 4.1 | 0 |
| 920930 | 0.00 | 131992.50 | 131992.50 | 5700.00 | 5.0 | 8.1 | 0 |
| 921231 | 0.00 | 135257.50 | 135257.50 | 5700.00 | 4.9 | 2.5 | 0 |

You could have one account trade both of these, but you would like to see what the implications would be of putting them together.

Figure 22 shows what happens when all of those four commodities are trading the One Night Stand simultaneously. It looks very similar to the British Pound trading alone. It is right 68 percent of the time, and it makes $97,000. The drawdown is $5,900, and there were 20 winners in a row.

This is very powerful.

One Night Stand has entries, exits, and stops. It has an entry system that I call Easy Moving Average, which is not even a moving average! It has an exit rule to get out at the very next opening, and we has no stops turned on.

To show you how to edit this model, I'm going to use the data on one commodity and run a quick test on one market. Using British Pound, I will now do a five-year test on the SystemWriter. I want to tell you the rules of One Night Stand, so you can get a feel for this system.

One Night Stand buys the highest high of the last four days if the 10-day moving average is above the 40-day moving average, and the program sells the lowest low of the last eight days if the 10-day moving average is lower than the 40-day moving average. We only trade it on a Friday, and we get out on Monday's opening! The idea behind this system is that currencies tend to breakout on the weekend, and people are afraid to take breakouts over the weekends. They are afraid of world events and they are afraid of the news.

Whatever people are afraid to do is probably what you should do. Basically, you are paying the margin, and taking

FIGURE 22
ONE NIGHT STAND

ONE NIGHT STAND 01/04/88 to 12/31/92 C:\PA\
BP1(1) 2700 DM1(1) 2700 SF1(1) 2700 JY1(1) 2700

| | | | |
|---|---|---|---|
| Total net profit | 97,037.50 | < 147,037.50> | |
| Gross profit | 131,586.25 | Gross loss | -34,548.75 |
| Total # of trades | 285 | Percent profitable | 68% |
| Number winning trades | 194 | Number losing trades | 91 |
| Largest winning trade | 3,070.00 | Largest losing trade | -2,267.50 |
| Average winning trade | 678.28 | Average losing trade | -379.66 |
| Ratio avg win/avg loss | 1.79 | Avg trade (win & loss) | 340.48 |
| Max consecutive winners | 20 | Max consecutive losers | 5 |
| Avg # bars in winners | 1 | Avg # bars in losers | 1 |
| Max drawdown | 5,912.50 | Avg # of contracts held | 2 |
| Profit factor | 1.22 | Max # of contracts held | 4 |
| Account size required | 16,712.50 | Return on account | 581% |

FIGURE 23
PERFORMANCE SUMMARY OF BRITISH POUND

| | | | |
|---|---|---|---|
| Max closed-out drawdown | $-2,145.00 | Max intra-day drawdown | $-2,145.00 |
| Profit factor | 3.24 | Max # of contracts held | 1 |
| Account size required | $5,145.00 | Return on account | 304% |

Highlights - Long trades

| Description | Date | Time | | Amount |
|---|---|---|---|---|
| Largest Winning Trade | 12/23/91 | - | $ | 2,232.50 |
| Largest Losing Trade | 10/07/91 | - | $ | -1,167.50 |
| Largest String of + Trades | 09/09/91 | - | | 14 |
| Largest String of - Trades | 12/18/89 | - | | 3 |
| Maximum Closed-Out Drawdown | 12/18/89 | - | $ | -2,145.00 |
| Maximum Intra-Day Drawdown | 12/18/89 | - | $ | -2,145.00 |

////////////////////////// SHORT TRADES - Test 1 \\\\\\\\\\\\\\\\\\\\\\\\\\

| | | | |
|---|---|---|---|
| Total net profit | $20,928.75 | | |
| Gross profit | $26,111.25 | Gross loss | $-5,182.50 |
| Total # of trades | 33 | Percent profitable | 72% |
| Number winning trades | 24 | Number losing trades | 9 |
| Largest winning trade | $3,020.00 | Largest losing trade | $-2,267.50 |
| Average winning trade | $1,087.97 | Average losing trade | $ -575.83 |
| Ratio avg win/avg loss | 1.88 | Avg trade (win & loss) | $634.20 |
| Max consecutive winners | 12 | Max consecutive losers | 3 |
| Avg # bars in winners | 1 | Avg # bars in losers | 1 |
| Max closed-out drawdown | $-2,535.00 | Max intra-day drawdown | $-2,535.00 |
| Profit factor | 5.03 | Max # of contracts held | 1 |
| Account size required | $5,535.00 | Return on account | 378% |

Highlights - Short trades

| Description | Date | Time | | Amount |
|---|---|---|---|---|
| Largest Winning Trade | 06/27/88 | - | $ | 3,020.00 |
| Largest Losing Trade | 09/06/88 | - | $ | -2,267.50 |
| Largest String of + Trades | 02/24/92 | - | | 12 |
| Largest String of - Trades | 06/20/88 | - | | 3 |
| Maximum Closed-Out Drawdown | 09/19/88 | - | $ | -2,535.00 |
| Maximum Intra-Day Drawdown | 09/19/88 | - | $ | -2,535.00 |

\\\\\\\\\\\\\\\\\\\\\\\\\\\\\\\\\\\\\\\\\\\\\\\\\\\\\\\\\\\\\\\\\\\\\\\\\\\\\\////////////////////////////////////

Prepared using System Writer Plus Version 2.18 by Omega Research, Inc.

the risk over the weekend. Figure 23 is a test done for the five-year period.

### One Night Stand's Track Record

It made $36,000. It was right 71 percent of the time, and there were 82 trades in five years. The average trade of a winner was $827. The average trade of a loser was $529. And the Daddy-go-to-town number was $394. It had a $2,600 draw-down. There were 20 consecutive winners, and four consecutive losers. (See Figure 24.)

Here are the longs. It is a balanced system. The long side made $15,000 with 49 trades. The short side made $16,000 with 33 trades. Even though the British Pound in the last five years has been fairly directional, here is a system that only carries positions over the weekend when no one else will carry them.

## PORTANA

The next program is a product called Portana, by Tom Berry Software. The idea here is to take output from SystemWriter Plus and say, "I like these systems, but what if I want to handle a bunch of them at a time?

What if I want to handle the Swiss Franc, the British Pound, and the Deutsche Mark, simultaneously? What will that do?"

With Portana we will import some files, and we will go down to where it says British Pound 1, which is One Night Stand, Japanese Yen 1, Deutsche Mark 1, and Swiss Franc I. We will

FIGURE 24
BRITISH POUND LONG TRADES

////////////////////////////////////////\\\\\\\\\\\\\\\\\\\\\\\\\\\\\\\\\\\\\\\

Directory : F:\KK Printed on : 10/03/93 11:25am

PERFORMANCE SUMMARY

| | | | |
|---|---|---|---|
| Model Name | : One Night Stand | Developer | : Krutsinger |
| Test Number | : 1 of 1 | | |

Notes : Combo Of MA and Channel Breakout, in on Fri. -Out on Mon.

| | |
|---|---|
| Data | : BRITISH POUND 06/93 |
| Calc Dates | : 01/01/88 - 12/31/92 |

| Num. | Conv. | P. Value | Comm | Slippage | Margin | Format | Drive:\Path\FileName |
|---|---|---|---|---|---|---|---|
| 26 | 2 | $ 6.250 | $ 55 | $ 0 | $ 3,000 | Omega | F:\20DATA06\F008.DTA |

////////////////////////////// ALL TRADES - Test 1 \\\\\\\\\\\\\\\\\\\\\\\\\\\\

| | | | |
|---|---|---|---|
| Total net profit | $36,615.00 | | |
| Gross profit | $48,798.75 | Gross loss | $-12,183.75 |
| Total # of trades | 82 | Percent profitable | 71% |
| Number winning trades | 59 | Number losing trades | 23 |
| Largest winning trade | $3,020.00 | Largest losing trade | $-2,267.50 |
| Average winning trade | $827.10 | Average losing trade | $ -529.73 |
| Ratio avg win/avg loss | 1.56 | Avg trade (win & loss) | $446.52 |
| Max consecutive winners | 20 | Max consecutive losers | 4 |
| Avg # bars in winners | 1 | Avg # bars in losers | 1 |
| Max closed-out drawdown | $-2,625.00 | Max intra-day drawdown | $-2,887.50 |
| Profit factor | 4.00 | Max # of contracts held | 1 |
| Account size required | $5,887.50 | Return on account | 621% |

Highlights - All trades

| Description | Date | Time | Amount |
|---|---|---|---|
| Largest Winning Trade | 06/27/88 | - | $ 3,020.00 |
| Largest Losing Trade | 09/06/88 | - | $ -2,267.50 |
| Largest String of + Trades | 09/09/91 | - | 20 |
| Largest String of - Trades | 06/20/88 | - | 4 |
| Maximum Closed-Out Drawdown | 05/11/92 | - | $ -2,625.00 |
| Maximum Intra-Day Drawdown | 05/15/92 | - | $ -2,887.50 |

////////////////////////////// LONG TRADES - Test 1 \\\\\\\\\\\\\\\\\\\\\\\\\\\\

| | | | |
|---|---|---|---|
| Total net profit | $15,686.25 | | |
| Gross profit | $22,687.50 | Gross loss | $-7,001.25 |
| Total # of trades | 49 | Percent profitable | 71% |
| Number winning trades | 35 | Number losing trades | 14 |
| Largest winning trade | $2,232.50 | Largest losing trade | $-1,167.50 |
| Average winning trade | $648.21 | Average losing trade | $ -500.09 |
| Ratio avg win/avg loss | 1.29 | Avg trade (win & loss) | $320.13 |
| Max consecutive winners | 14 | Max consecutive losers | 3 |
| Avg # bars in winners | 1 | Avg # bars in losers | 1 |

make sure we do not have anything else, because Portana is very powerful. You can add one hundred different systems simultaneously!

I am going to have these four commodities–the BP, the JY, the SF, and the DM. I previously ran these on SystemWriter, and just dumped them on a file. Portana will read the SystemWriter file directly, so I don't have to re-run them. (See Figure 25.)

Portana processes five years of trading on all of these commodities, laying them together, and showing us how they would come out. This is a very powerful tool.

## Benefit of Portana

Here is the most powerful feature of Portana: You can get reports that will show you monthly, daily, and quarterly where you would be. I am going to show you a graph now that is incredible. This is the daily equity graph. It shows you what would happen if you traded all four currencies simultaneously. Then it shows you day by day what your equity would be and what your maximum drawdown would be. (See Figure 26.)

The bottom line is your maximum drawdown, which is $5,900. The only line is $97,000, which is your profits. You can look at it day by day by day and see your equity curve. The closer to a 45-degree angle your equity curve is, the better your system is. What you want to look at, when you are analyzing systems, are the times of drawdown. Figure 26 (page 49) shows the places where periods of drawdown occur. Can you stand those? Then you may have a winning piece of strategy.

FIGURE 25
PORTFOLIO ANALYZER — PORTANA

PORTFOLIO ANALYZER YEARLY REPORT for ONE NIGHT STAND

| DATE | OPEN EQUITY | CLOSED EQUITY | TOTAL EQUITY | MAX DRAWDOWN | STAND % DD | % CHNG TOT EQ | NUM TRADE |
|---|---|---|---|---|---|---|---|
| 880104 | 0.00 | 50000.00 | 50000.00 | 0.00 | 0.0 | 0.0 | 0 |
| 881230 | 0.00 | 59317.50 | 59317.50 | 5912.50 | 11.8 | 18.6 | 0 |
| 891229 | 0.00 | 73425.00 | 73425.00 | 5912.50 | 11.8 | 23.8 | 0 |
| 901231 | 0.00 | 94432.50 | 94432.50 | 5912.50 | 11.8 | 28.6 | 0 |
| 911231 | 0.00 | 127822.50 | 127822.50 | 5912.50 | 7.6 | 35.4 | 0 |
| 921231 | 0.00 | 147037.50 | 147037.50 | 5912.50 | 6.1 | 15.0 | 0 |

FIGURE 26
PORTFOLIO ANALYZER FOR TEST

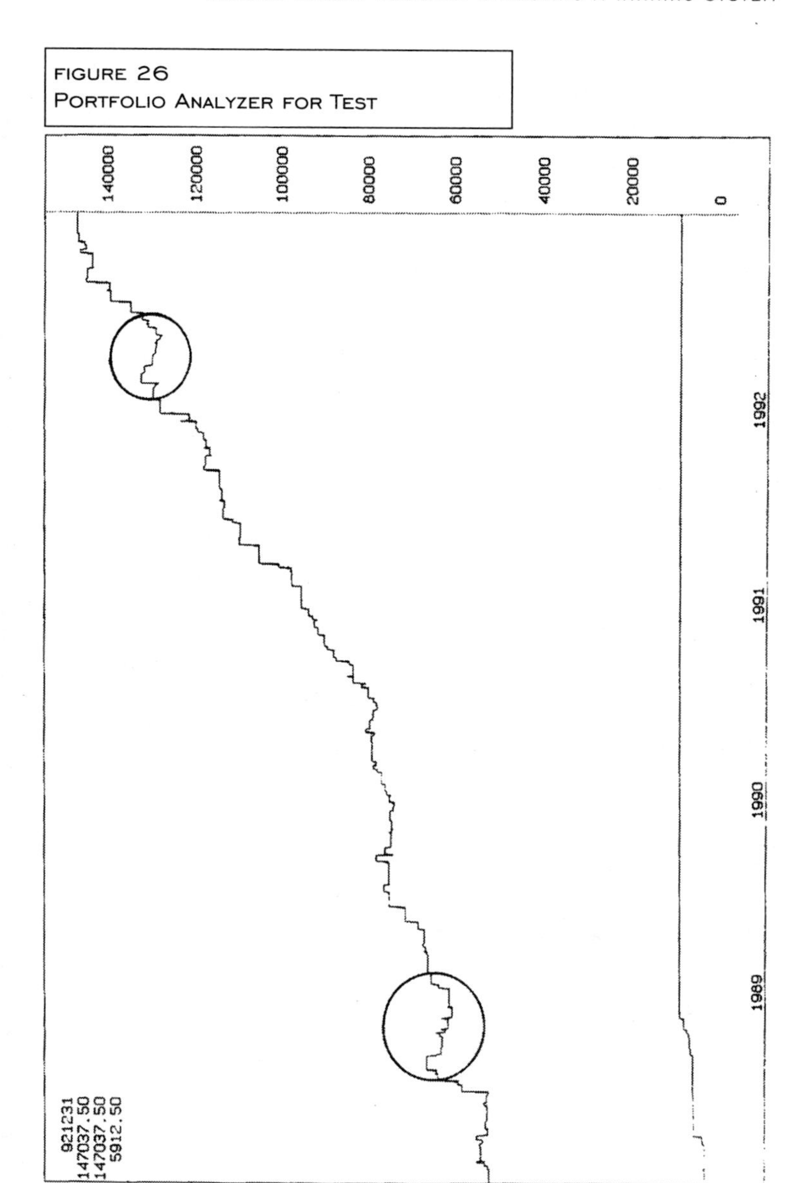

# ONE DAY AT A TIME

The last piece of software I want you to see is a product called One Day at a Time; it is more a trading tool. It is a product written by Wells Wilder that came into use as a game. As you actually look at the markets it will hold off on some of the bars that are there and show you just a few of the bars at a time. Your goal is to make trading decisions based on what you see. It is a beautiful charting package. I just want you to see how easy it is to use.

Figure 27 is a chart of the S&P in a daily mode through December 1992 on daily bars. I have elected to see the moon phases. It shows me when there is a full moon and when there is a half moon. If I wanted to see candlestick charts I would touch the T key for Japanese Yen, and then hit candlestick charts. (See Figure 28.)

If I wanted to do one of Wells Wilder's models, which is called an Adam Projection (a very high level piece of math that projects where it thinks the market is going to go in the next few bars), I would hit the letter A and One Day at a Time would project where that piece of math would put the market in the next few days. (See Figure 29.)

If I wanted to see weekly charts, I'd just hit the W, and One Day at a Time would change all that data to weekly data (Figure 30).

If I wanted to see monthly charts, I would hit the W one more time (Figure 31).

My machine, by the way, is a 386-20, which is very low tech now. Three years ago it was state-of-the-art. So it's a little slower

FIGURE 27
CHART OF S&P DAILY MODE

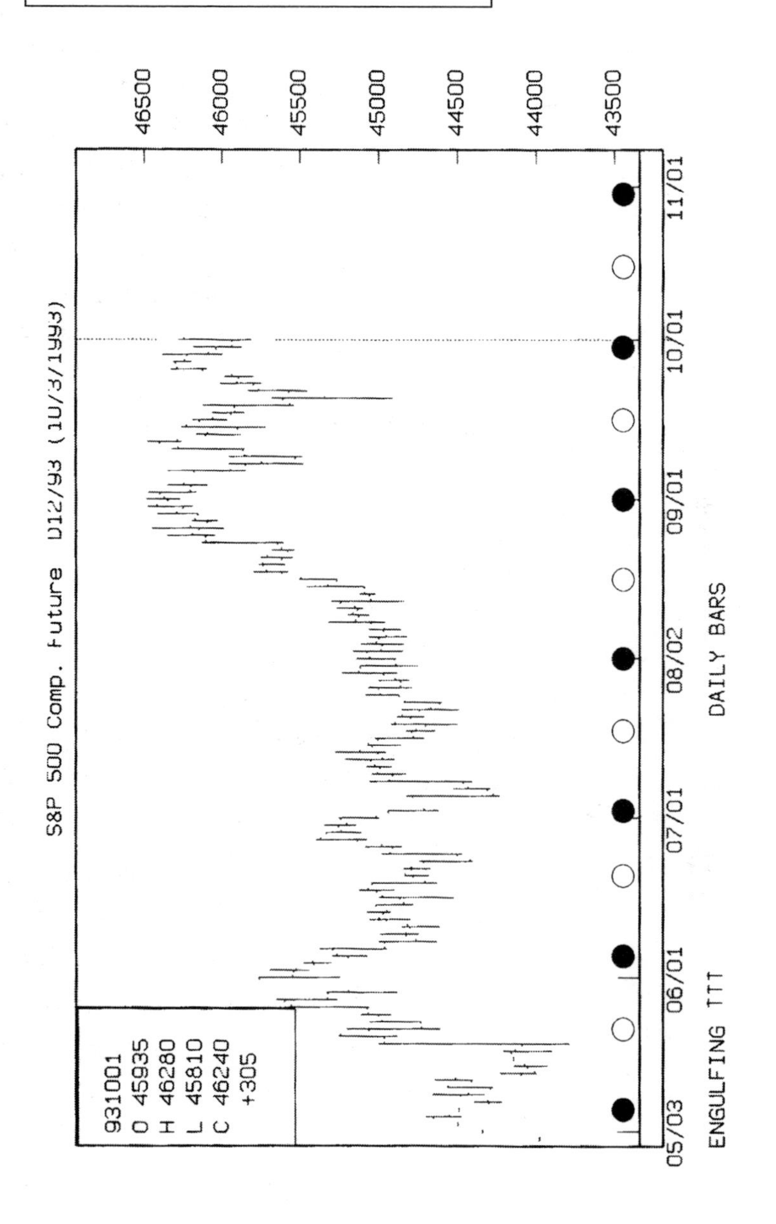

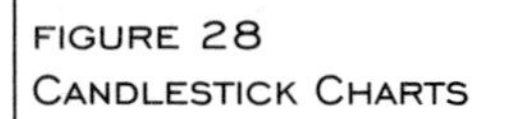

FIGURE 28
CANDLESTICK CHARTS

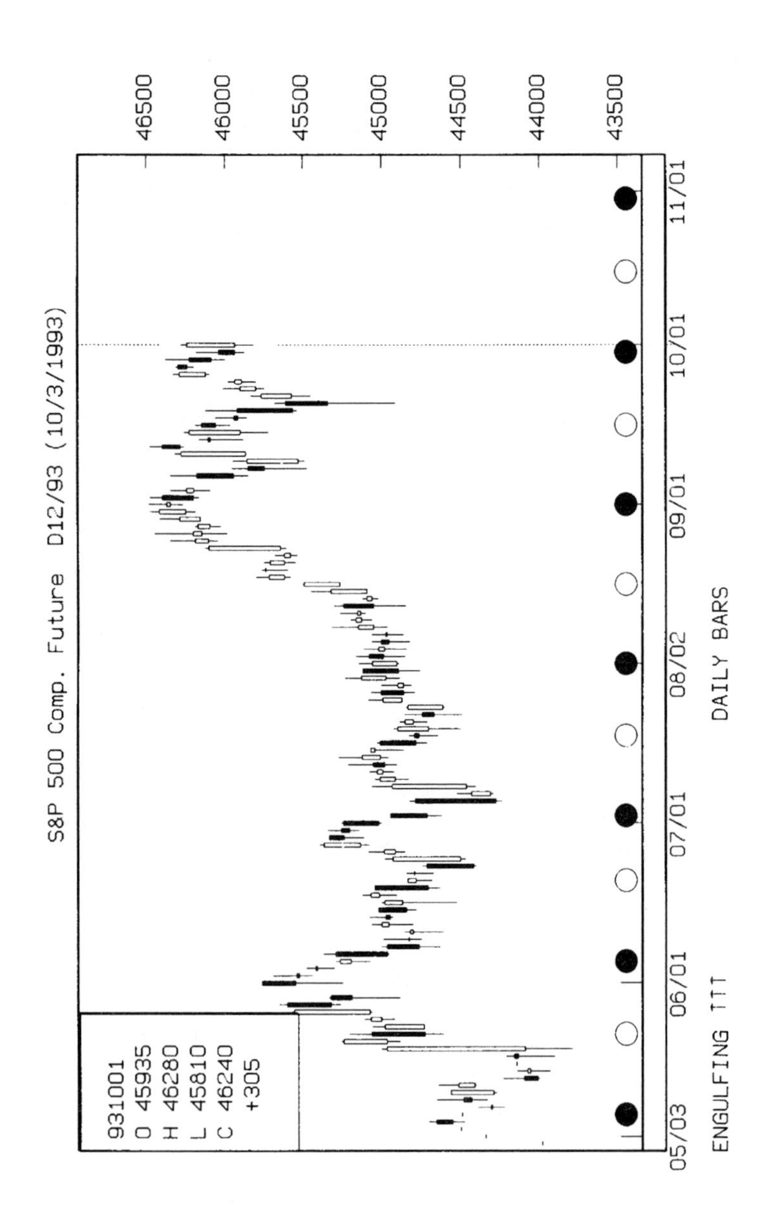

FIGURE 29
Daily Bars — (Adam Projection)

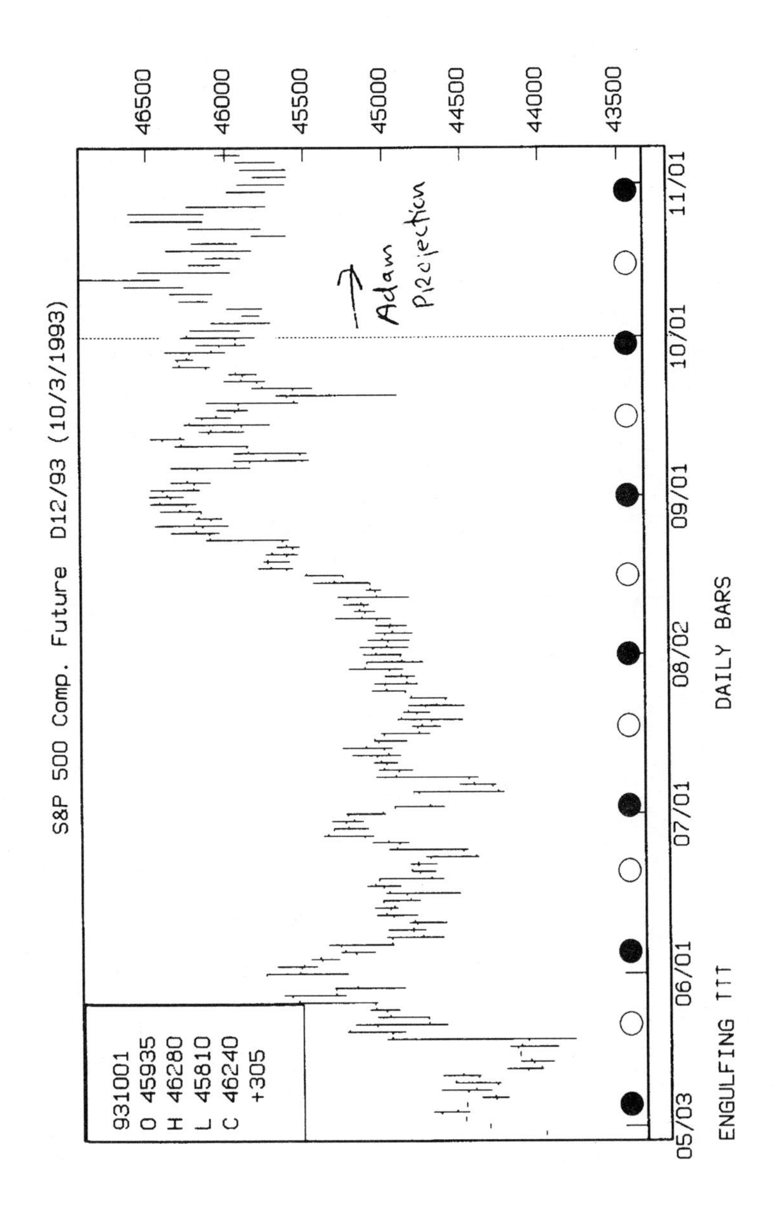

FIGURE 30
Weekly Bars

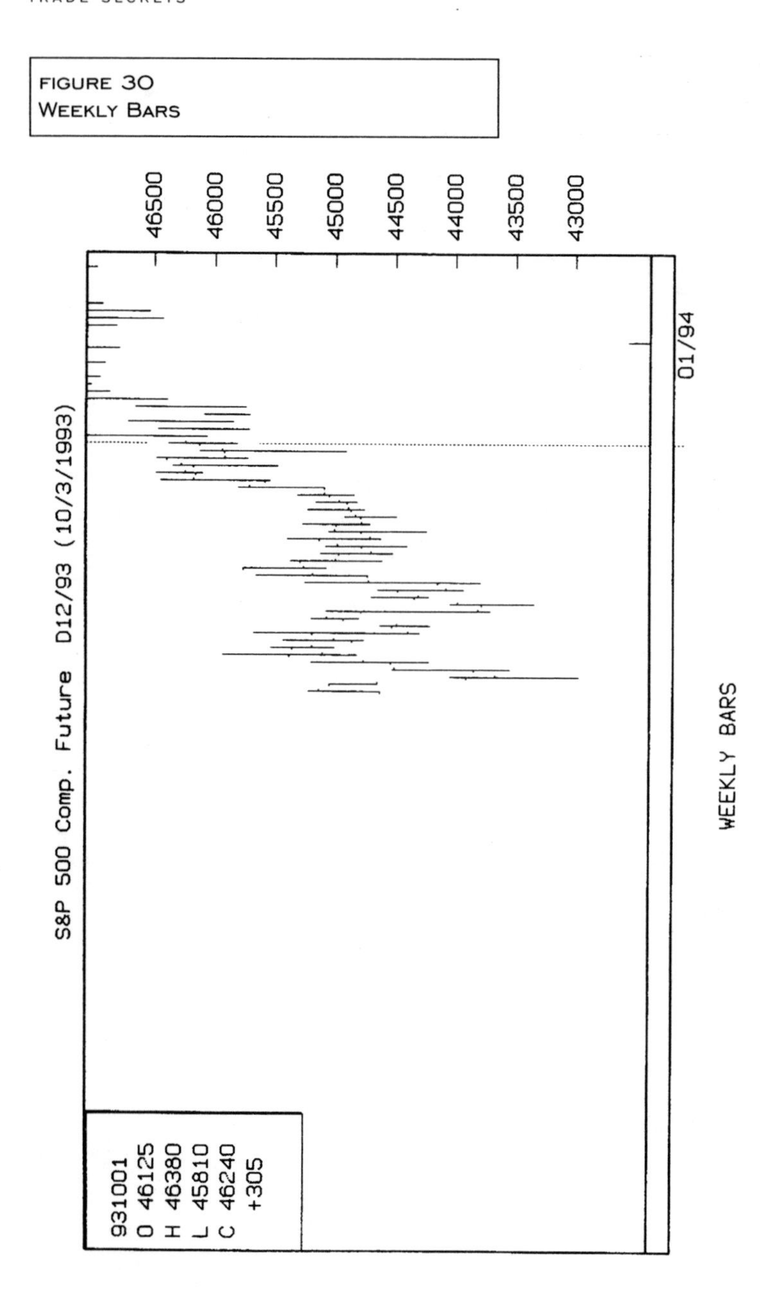

FIGURE 31
MONTHLY BARS

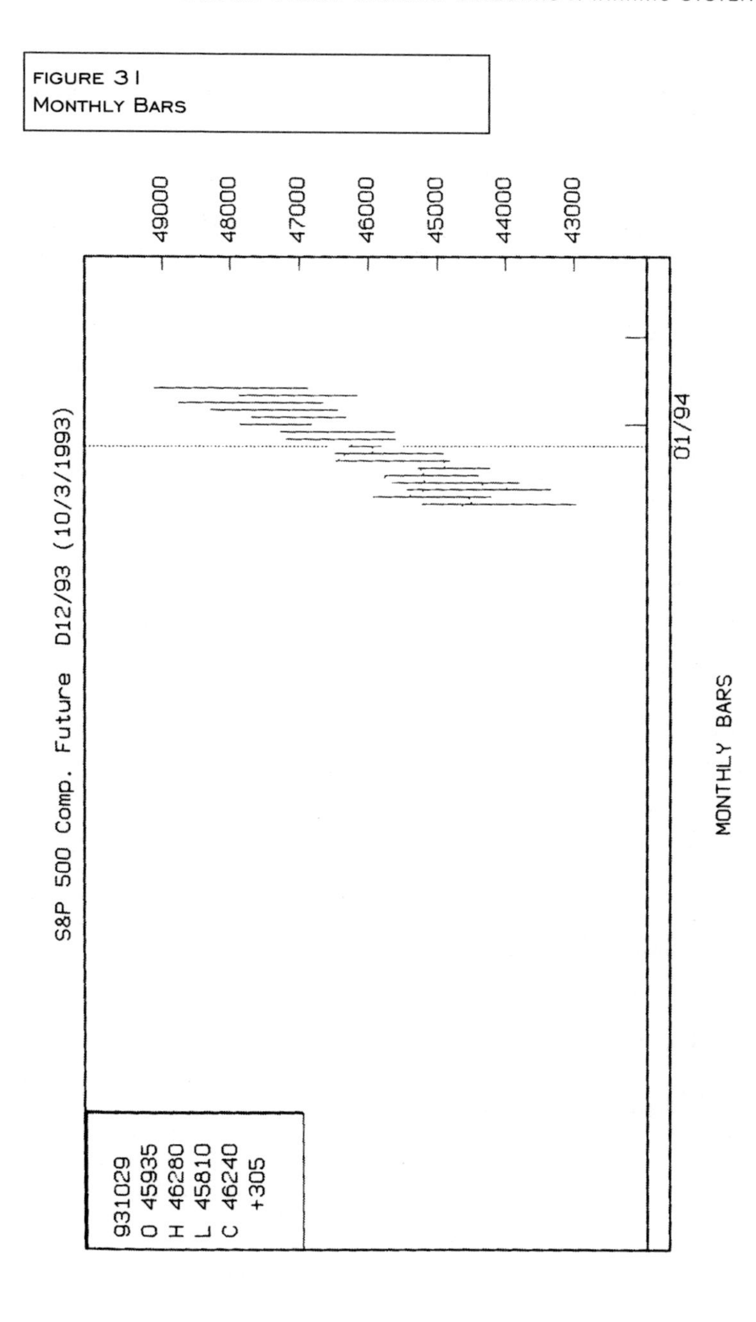

than the one on your desk. Here we have monthly bars of the S&P back through 1984 in candlestick format with an Adam Projection, and I never use more than one finger. One Day at a Time is a very good system for someone who is trying to learn the markets and learn how to manipulate data.

## IMPLEMENTATION

The power of using your system or any system rests in your implementation. The key is not in the writing or the testing of a system, but it is in implementing it every day. You will forget to run your numbers if you are trading a third-party system or you will look at a trade and say, "I do not want to do that. There is a report coming out next Tuesday, and I do not want to be in that position," or you will say, "It's been too choppy lately. I don't want to trade the dollar index." You will defeat your own system.

You can get the best system I develop, the best system you develop, the best system Wells Wilder develops, but if you don't follow the rules explicitly the way they were written and tested, you will not have a system.

## PLAN YOUR STRATEGY, THEN FOLLOW YOUR PLAN

Take, for example, the Buy Monday plan, discussed earlier in this chapter.

Here is the entry rule. If it is Monday, buy it. I will repeat that. If it is Monday, buy it. Here is the exit rule. Get out on the close on Monday. We are trading S&P, and we will buy it every Monday. We will put in a $500 stop, and we will get out on Monday's close.

I have given this same system in many seminars around the country.

People invariably call me up and say, "I tried your system and it didn't work." I say, "Oh, really?" (By the way, it only works half the time, so it is logical that this would happen.) I will ask the client, "How did you do it?"

"Well, last Tuesday I bought it, and then I got out and I lost money."

"Last Tuesday!" I would reiterate. "But the system says to buy on Monday. It is a very simple S&P system. You put in a $500 stop, and you get out on the close. Why didn't you buy it on Monday?"

"We weren't open Monday."

The point is: It doesn't matter how simple a system is. If you do not implement it correctly, then you really do not have a system. I think this is an extreme example, but if someone can foul up a system like this, think about what they can do with three or four pages of Fortran or C Programming.

# An Interview with Joe Krutsinger

Joe Krutsinger is President of Krutsinger & Krutsinger, Inc., an Omega Solution provider and software publishing firm that distributes and supports Portana, the Portfolio Analyzer Software developed by Tom Berry and Welles Wilder. He is also the Trading Systems Designer for Robbins Trading Company in Chicago and has years of experience developing and testing trade system ideas. He has traveled the country showing traders how to systemize their trading and is the instructor of the popular video series, *Trading System Development*. Joe also is the author of the *Trading Systems Toolkit*.

**1** Tell me about yourself: If someone were to say, "Tell me about Joe Krutsinger," what would you want them to know? Give me a brief biography of you before you got into commodities, and a brief biography of what you have done since you got into commodities.

**Joe** Before I was in commodities, I was in the grocery business. I went to Michigan State University, and I was the outstanding senior in food systems, economics and management. Michigan State is a pretty big campus, had 43,000 students, so that made me feel pretty good. I was loading block salt one day, and a farmer dropped a block of salt and mashed my hand; he didn't say excuse me or anything, he just kept on loading. I said to myself, gee, I think I've taken a wrong career path. So with my broken hand, I decided to get into commodities, and I went to look at commodity firms.

As far as what I've done since I've gotten into commodities, in 1978 I became the youngest vice president of Piper Jeffrey and Hopwood. In 1980 I had 16 job offers, all of them in Des Moines, Iowa, to run commodity departments. The commodity field is fairly small, and I think I have done fairly well in it. I have been a broker continuously since 1976. This is my 21st year in commodities.

**2** Tell me about your technique. What makes it exclusively yours? How did you develop it?

**Joe** Actually, my technique is using software developed by others. I've become an expert at System Writer, TradeStation, Super Charts, and Portana. I liked Portana so much I bought the company. I am not a software designer, but I am a very good software user, and basically my technique is to use commercial software.

**3** Tell me about your best current trading system. What makes it tick? What are the features that make it the best trading system? Why do you trade this system?

**Joe** The best current trading system I have is actually One Night Stand, and I wrote it in 1992. It's actually a world famous system. There are over 50,000 copies in circulation. When I wrote the system One Night Stand, I had showed it to *Futures Magazine*, and they put it in their "Trading Systems Special Issue." They printed up 50,000 copies of that special issue and distributed it to about everybody in commodities. The interesting thing about One Night Stand is that I divulged all the rules. The entry, the exit if you are right, the exit if you are wrong, and although it has had wide distribution, the system continues to do well today.

**4** How long ago did you write your first trading system?

**Joe** The first trading system I can remember writing was in 1979, called Hi Ho Silver, and basically it's this: If the close is above the 32 day moving average, you're long; if it's below it, you're short. Remember, in 1979, there weren't many people writing trading systems, and in a five year period, that system made over a quarter of a million dollars trading just silver.

**5** Remember back to your first trading system. Call you tell us the rules?

**Joe** I just gave you the rules on Hi Ho Silver, which basically is: If the price is above the 32 day moving average, you're long silver; if it's below it, you're short. You're always in the market.

**6** What caused you to abandon or modify that trading system the very first time?

**Joe** I decided to look for more complicated trading systems, thinking that surely complication was the key. I used a variation of this system in cattle. In 1983, I had nine losing trades in a row, always reversing, always being on one side of the market or the other in a reversal system, and although the tenth trade was a huge winner. It made me kind of wonder about reversal systems.

**7** When you look at another person's trading system, what is the very first thing you look for to tell if it's a good or a bad system?

**Joe** Drawdown. If the drawdown is too big, you'll never trade that system, at least not for very long. That is the very most important thing to look at, the magnitude of the drawdown.

8 What is the least important aspect of a trading system as far as you are concerned?

Joe Consecutive winners or consecutive losers. A lot of people put a lot of store in that, but I had a real-time trading system in 1989 that had 42 consecutive winners, and then I had a loser, and 25 percent of my people quit because they thought the system was broken. So consecutive winners or losers don't mean much to me anymore.

9 In your current work, are you using a mechanical approach or is there a judgment involved in your trading ?

Joe I use 100 percent mechanical systems. My idea of a great system is: A system that once I write it, I never have to touch it again–One Night Stand, Paul Revere. Paul Revere is a trading system for the British pound where you buy at the highest high of the last six days, or sell to the lowest low of the last six days, and use $1,000 stop. I haven't changed the rules for Paul Revere since I wrote it in 1989.

**10** Are you currently using TradeStation or SystemWriter? If not, what software do you use to run your trading system?

**Joe** I use all the Omega products. System Writer, I still think, is the very best tool if you are looking for what combination of systems will work the best. Because you can still take several pieces of data and ten or twelve different trading systems, and let the machine sort out the body, so to speak. TradeStation isn't to that order of effectiveness, yet.

**11** Is your current trading system for sale? For lease? On a fax line? How do you provide this information to clients?

**Joe** My current trading system is a bond system that I lease for $75 a month per contract trade. The reason I lease it for such a small amount of money is that I want to lease a lot of them, and as people have experience with the system, instead of trading one contract or two contracts, I hope they trade four or five. If a person trades four con-

**tracts on my system, he has to pay me $300 a month. I trade all my systems exclusively at Robbins Trading, where I'm a consultant, so that I can watch my systems and tune them up, and make sure they are being traded correctly.**

12

Can you share the concept behind your trading system, for example, your main entry technique, your exit if you are wrong, and your exit if you are right?

Joe

**The rules to One Night Stand, which I think is my best system, are basically this. If the ten day moving average is above the 40 and today is Friday, then buy the highest high of the last four days on the stock. If the ten day is below the 40 and today is Friday, then sell if the lowest low of the last 8 days on the stop. Use $1,000 stop on day of entry, and get out on Monday's opening. The system is so hard to do in real time because no one wants to buy new highs and sell new lows going into a weekend, carry the position and then automatically liquidate. It's very, very difficult to get someone to actually do it.**

As far as the current system I'm using at Robbins, it is a volatility breakout system on bonds. It has a day trade module and an overnight module, and the concept is to hold bonds for a very short length of time, but overnight. Hold them for a day or two to make probably ten or twelve trades a month on the overnight system, another eight or nine trades a month in the day trade system, and try to make between $6,000 and $8,000 a year per contract traded. That's very good return in bonds, and that is my goal.

13

If you could advise system developers to do one thing when they are starting out, what would that be?

Joe

I guess the first thing I would tell them to do is read the body of knowledge. For example, look at Larry Williams' work. Larry Williams, I think, is the very best system developer in the world. Look at some of the old work, lessons from the masters. Read the Jessie Livermore book, *Reminiscence of a Stock Operator*, and code some of that into a TradeStation and System Writer and see how well it works today, but don't get myopic looking at your own little thing. Look at other people's material. Code up what they have to say and see if there are things you can use.

**14**

Other than yourself; who do you think is the best system developer, or who do you think is the best teacher of system development?

**Joe**

Other than myself, huh! Well, actually I think the best system developer and best teacher are both Larry Williams. Larry is not only probably the nicest guy in the futures business, but also he's probably the smartest, and he is a very modest person. He is able to communicate at all levels. He's just an excellent, excellent person and system developer.

**15**

When you devise a trading system, what timeframe do you use most? For example, do you use daily bars, weekly bars, l-minute bars, 10-minute bars, or 60-minute bars?

**Joe**

I like daily bars. There are some problems with them, using close stops and some of the things, the intricacies for day trading. But you can get them readily, the data is clean, and you can be pretty sure if you've got a system that you've tested correctly on daily bars without too many parameters in it, you have a good chance of it repeating. One of the problems with small time frame stuff is you can find stuff that works over a three or four month period because of a unique way the market's running. For instance, here it is the first quarter of 1996, and you have a very volatile market in the stock market and the bond market, very high ranges. Stuff that you write and make work in this time frame may not work in most time frames.

**16**

If for some reason they closed every commodity in the world except one, and you were the guy in charge of deciding which one would stay open, which commodity would you choose? Why? What hours would it be open?

**Joe**

United States Treasury Bonds, and I would have them open from 8:00 A.M. until 2:00 P.M.

**17**

If you were to choose one commodity you could never trade again and you could never include in a trading system, which commodity would this be? Why?

**Joe**

I guess, if I had to say there is one commodity that I just could do without trading, it would be oats. I think you can fool yourself with oats about as well as anything because it's such a small contract, and it moves in such a small manner, you can sit in a position forever and never really get anywhere. As far as testing, there is not enough volatility. I think it's the kind of contract you could pretty well lead. There's an old phrase in commodities back from the early days that said, "Gentlemen don't trade oats."

**18**

Where do you get your ideas for your system? A chart? A pattern? Observations?' Trades that you have done before? What is your favorite technique for coming up with a trading system?

**Joe**

My favorite technique is to look at major tops and bottoms and draw out what is going on right before the top or bottom–in other words, patterns. I think indicators can be stressed way too much in most systems. My favorite systems have no indicators. They look at a pattern, and then they do a break out anticipating a trend change. Larry Williams' OOPS! system, when the market opens sharply lower and then comes back to the previous day's low, for instance, is a classic example of the kind of system that I think is unbeatable because you can see the market psychology there at work where the people say, "OOPS! Something is wrong," and they have to go back the other way.

**10**

I want you to write a trading system for me. I want you to give me all the rules. I want you to tell me what commodity, what time frame, whether it is daily bars, whatever. What your entry rule is, your exit rule with a profit, your exit rule with a loss. It doesn't have to be a great system. Just give me an idea of something you would look at, something you would test to see if there was any validity.

**Joe**

One of the things I'd look at is a dual system. A system where it does one thing in choppy markets and does another thing in trending markets. The trending part of the system would be fairly easy, something like this. Buy tomorrow at the highest high of the last 10 days on the stop; sell tomorrow at the lowest low of the last 10 days on the stop. Then I would also have a condition. And the condition would be if the range of today is less than the average range of the last 10 days, then I would trade System 1. If today's range is above the range of the last 10 days, then I would trade System 2. As far as exit with a loss, I would probably use a money management rule of about $500, and as far as exit with a profit, I would not use a profit target.

**20**

What's the typical day in the life of a system developer? What time do you start? What time do you end? What is it you do all day long? How are your orders placed? How is your system run?

**Joe**

Basically, I'm in the office before 7:00 A.M. to make sure all the data was collected right and all the systems are running. I'm fairly unusual because I have 18 different active trading systems to watch. I have eight TradeStations to monitor so mine is kind of a mechanical life. I want to make sure that those opening ticks come in right and everything is fine.

After all the openings are done by 9:30 A.M. Chicago time, I pretty well sit in a room and write new trading systems and work on new work. I'll be interrupted several times a day to help clients and prospects from all over the world tune up their trading systems, or figure out what it is they are trying to do. I eat lunch about 12:30, 12:45, and by 4:30, 5:00, I'm back home.

21

If you could have your system run in any manner what would be the preferable method? Would you have the person whose money is at risk run the system, or would you have a third party run the system and just arbitrarily take the trades as they are generated, regardless of consequence ?

Joe

I really prefer the system assisted approach that Robbins has; that's why I helped make it come to be. I feel that it's much easier for someone who doesn't have their money at risk, to follow the rules and to follow them correctly without trying to put judgment into the system. I think that's what made System Assist the success it is.

**22** Let's pretend I don't have a single book on commodities, and I'm interested in writing systems. Other than your own work, what book would you recommend? Along these same lines, is there anything you would avoid, whether it's software, books, lectures, whatever?

**Joe** I think Larry Williams' books, the *Silver Book* and the *Gold Book* are invaluable as are any of his seminar manuals. I think you can learn the most by writing systems, and the way you write systems is to look at other successful systems and build your own building blocks. As far as things to avoid, I think I would avoid a lot of the black box stuff—the stuff that's out there that you put in the open, high, low, and close and push a button, and it tells you something to do, but doesn't really tell you why. I would avoid that stuff.

23 Do you think it is necessary for a software developer/real-time trader to have tick-by-tick real-time quotes? Why or why not?

Joe I do not. I think the daily bar is enough, and I think if you want to back test and do some dual testing on back tick data to make sure that the daily bar acts the way you want, that's fine. But I think that watching the market is not beneficial at all.

24 What kind of quotes do you have? What kind of software would you recommend? Are there any systems or software that you would definitely not recommend?

Joe I use Signal and Bonneville quotes. I guess Signal has acquired Bonneville now. And I use TradeStation. If I were just watching quotes and not writing systems, Commodity Quotes Graphics is a tremendous piece of software. I had one of the very first ones in 1983, but since I am a system developer and write lots of trading systems, there is absolutely no platform better, that I know of, than Omega's TradeStation. I don't think

I'd recommend the systems that are the handheld variety. I've heard guys say they take them to the restroom at work and watch their handheld system and make trading decisions. I think that's a poor way to trade.

**25** How much data do you think is necessary to be tested as far as assessing a day-trade session on five-minute bars? A daily bar system? A 60-minute system?

**Joe** As far as a daily system, I think you have to have three years of data to show a test and three years of data on a daily system of 750 bars. I think 750 bars is a good length number of bars to test. In a 60-minute session that would be about 120 days or so, and so forth.

**26** Why do some systems consistently perform year after year, and other systems fail or need to be continually optimized?

**Joe** I think the more parameters there are in a system, the more likely it is to fail, and the more likely it is for those parameters to have to be analyzed.

If you have a basic pattern setup such as a higher high today and a lower low today than the previous day, that's an outside day setup. You take that, and then you can use a trigger; if tomorrow's low is below today's low, then sell. I think those types of things that are very hard to optimize to any degree tend to hold up.

27

How important are drawdowns in your research? How important is average trade size?

Joe

Drawdowns are the most important thing. When I look at total money made if the drawdown is more than 10 percent of the total money made, I don't like the system. As far as average trade size, the average winner or the average loser doesn't mean as much to me as the average trade. The average trade size should be over $150 in most systems. In bonds, I'll take a very small average trade size of $60 to $70 because the bonds have very little slippage.

**28** Do you do portfolio management—linking several commodities of different systems together? Do you do pyramiding? Why or why not?

**Joe** Absolutely. The only way to make a lot of money in commodities is to find systems that complement each other. I've done a lot of work on this. I have a program called All In One where I take One Night Stand, my S&P system, my bond system, blend them together and do them all in one. And that's really a huge new area of system development, portfolioing and pyramiding.

**29** Let's get a little morbid. You've died. You've left a sealed letter to your heirs. It contains the secret of your fortune. It's the secret to allow them to continue the lifestyle to which they have been accustomed. What one sentence is in the letter?

**Joe** Buy Monday, buy the S&P on Monday, use $1,000 stop, get out on the close. That is the secret.

30

Without giving the secret of life, how would you write an imitation of your system in two lines or less in TradeStation language? For example, I have an S&P system called Buy Monday. "Monday you buy it, put in a $1400 stop, get out on close." That's how you write that.

Joe

That's how I write it too! That's my Buy Monday system.

31

Give us an example of some of your work put in English-type language for a system.

Joe

I've given several of those, but I think the best thing you can do is take my Buy Monday together with my One Night Stand and then use a volatility breakout in bonds, and I'll give you the volatility breakout system in bonds. Buy tomorrow at the open tomorrow plus 30 percent of the range on the stop. Sell tomorrow at the open tomorrow minus 30 percent of the range on the stop. Use a $500 stop, and get out on the first possible opening.

# CONCLUSION

**AS WE REACH THE END,** I hope I've made it clear that there is no single secret to successful trading. You can experience tremendous success with a variety of systems, using a number of different software programs - or you can even apply the old "egg-timer" method - and still enjoy enormous profits.

You will, no doubt, also encounter disappointing periods in the course of your trading. It's the nature of the process - and it is to be expected.

However, the main point I've wanted to covey with this guide is that traders who are consistently successful over time are the ones that have a trading system that works for them. It's a system they believe in and can implement with complete confidence. Their system will surely incorporate guidelines that let traders hang onto winning trades, allowing profits to grow - while also showing how to take losses quickly and with few regrets. A system that does this will have you on the winning side of the fence far more often. And that's the real goal here - to have your system, the one you are most comfortable with, increase your percentage of wins.

Now that we've covered many of the basics needed for evaluating, testing and selecting the appropriate trading system for your needs, you'll have to decide how active a trader you'll want to be. Will you want to be glued to your computer screen - watching the market tick by tick? Will you be a more casual, occasional trader? Or a beeper-carrying trader that needs to be alerted as soon as the market makes a critical move?

I have developed a unique product called the Bail Suite, described in the back of the book, which I feel allows users to trade daily - while only spending minimal time monitoring the market. I refer to it as a "white box" system, rather than the dominant "black box" ones on the market. Other systems are designed for varying levels of involvement. The overriding point here is: What suits your temperament? Your needs? Your schedule? Can you handle the daily volatility? Do you have the discipline to avoid reacting to the day's events - and stick with your game plan?

These are questions that can be answered only by you. But, it is my hope that this book has empowered you to discover these answers on your own, so you can become a better, more consistent and more profitable trader. And I hope I've inspired you to continue the exciting challenges trading presents. It's an exhilarating, often frustrating yet highly intoxicating process. And, with all the latest technological advances - trading has never been more accessible to the individual. But, the basic foundations of every successful trader - large or small, individual or institutional - remain virtually the same. And right up at the top of the list is finding, testing and using a trading system that is appropriate for you.

Once you've done this - you're on your way. Enjoy the adventure!

# Trading Resource Guide

❖

## Tools for Successful Trading

## If you own Trading Systems Secrets ...

**Deduct $15 when you buy either one of Joe Krutsinger's bestselling books....**

> "When I have problems writing systems, I call Joe ...Now you get to tap into his great knowledge."
>
> \- Larry Williams, *How I Made $1 Million Trading Commodities*

## Buy *Trading Systems Toolkit* and Save $15!

### Trading Systems Toolkit

**Save $15**

**Joe Krutsinger $55.00 - $15 = $40 Item #3567**

This top selling book covers everything you need to use - or build - profitable trading systems. First, Krutsinger describes his favorite proven systems - the One Night Stand system, the Fib Catcher, etc. Then, he shows you how to create your own system. It's all here: entry & exit signals, where to place protective stops, when to get out, calculate drawdown and how to tailor a system to your own needs. A top seller.

**OR ...**

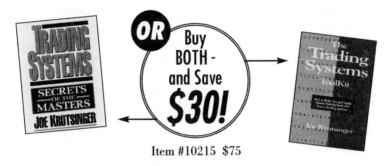

## SUGGESTED READING LIST

**DESIGN, TESTING & OPTIMIZATION OF TRADING SYSTEMS,** *Robert Pardo,* Hands on guide to building, refining and trading your own computerized trading system. Regardless of which technical software you use, you'll learn to choose the right indicators to suit your risk tolerance and profit goals. Discover how to combine a wide range of indicators and analysis methods to compliment each other. Pardo, a pioneer in trading system development, walks you through the process of refining, testing and trading your chosen system.
164 PP $45.00 ITEM #2171

**WINNING MARKET SYSTEMS,** *Gerald Appel,* Top trader Appel introduces little-known systems of the world's best traders. Get full details of each system and explanations on how to interpret & apply them to your trading. Plus concise rules for interpreting 83 systems including Larry William's accumulation-distribution formula, Zweig's Option-Activity ratio, Arm's short term trading index (Trin) and more. 223 PP $49.95 ITEM #2166

**STREET SMARTS:** *High Probability Trading Strategies for the Futures and Equities Markets, Linda Bradford Raschke & Larry Connors,* Two top selling authors and master traders team up to write a manual every serious trader should own. Profit-packed strategies are revealed, plus, chapters on volatility, reverse logic, trading pattern recognition, trading the smart money index and tons of other strategies. Given the best 4- star rating by Commodity Traders Consumer Reports - it's simply one of the best manuals on short term trading. Don't miss it. 237 PP $175 ITEM #5143

**TRADING THE PLAN:** *Build Wealth, Manage Money, Control Risk, Robert Deel,* How much should you risk in any one trade? How much leverage should you use? Answers to these & other tough questions on investing, managing money and limiting profit-draining losses.
220 PP $49.95 ITEM #6979

**NEW MARKET WIZARDS,** *Jack Schwager,* Meet a new generation of market killers. These winning traders make millions - often in hours - and consistently outperform peers. Trading across a spectrum of financial markets, they use different methods but share remarkable successes. How do they do it? How can you do it?? Learn their successful trading tactics.

493 PP $39.95 ITEM #2106

**MARKET WIZARDS,** *Jack Schwager,* How do the world's top traders amass millions? This classic bestseller takes you into the minds of the greatest traders Wall St. has ever known. In depth interviews with key players expose every facet of their strategies, making this an investment "Bible."

458 PP $22.95 ITEM #2241

ALSO AVAILABLE IN SOFTCOVER - $15 ITEM #2243

**TRADING SYSTEMS & METHODS, 3RD EDITION,** *Perry J. Kaufman,* It's the bestselling guide to trading systems – newly updated and revised with the current, cutting-edge material and a hands-on look at the good and bad features of most trading techniques and systems. Covers the latest, most successful indicators, programs, algorithms and systems. Plus, an update on new equipment and methods for trading. From neural nets, genetic algorithms, to spreadsheets, programs and other useful tools – it's the single best source for creating or choosing a successful trading system.

350 PP ITEM #8791 $79.95

**HOW I MADE 1 MILLION TRADING COMMODITIES,** *Larry Williams,* The pros have an unerring ability to forecast where prices are headed, enabling them to grab big profits. So supertrader Williams developed a system to detect what the pros were doing - and when. By following their moves - seeing when they're long/short, when they expect a major move - anyone can make their own trades profitable. It's an uncomplicated system that follows the money - and has worked consistently. Here's a chance to learn this phenomenal system - and start making your own million.

130 PP $55.00 ITEM #2606

**SURE THING COMMODITY TRADING,** *Plus Update, Larry Williams*
A major breakthrough in successful commodity trading. Features a systematic trading program with documented proof that 7 winners out of every 8 seasonal tendency commodity trades achieved an amazing $687,942 gain. The Update tracks every trade up-to-the minute- and shows that the system still works in the 90s.

200 PP $60.00 ITEM #2556

**THE SECRET OF SELECTING STOCKS FOR IMMEDIATE AND SUBSTANTIAL GAIN,** *Larry Williams,* Learn how top trader Williams identifies stocks that are under professional scrutiny and how to use that information to jump on market trends as they develop. Combine his timing rules with stock selection for even better profits.

114 PP $25.00 ITEM #2818

**DEFINITIVE GUIDE TO FUTURES TRADING,** *Volume 1, Larry Williams,* He won the *World Cup Championship of Futures Trading* and now he reveals the winning methods he pioneered. Both the accumulation/distribution method and %R method revolutionized the futures industry, and he discusses them in detail along with price pattern rules, forecasting methods, and 6 profitable stock index futures trading methods.

292 PP $55.00 ITEM #2586

**DEFINITIVE GUIDE TO FUTURES TRADING,** *Volume 2, Larry Williams,* Concluding volume of Williams' revolutionary work. Includes 50 pages of Larry's personal day trading knowledge. A money management technique to give you 99% probability of doubling your money. The Ultimate Oscillator, the Zero Balance method & loads of usable hands-on trading strategy.

274 PP $55.00 ITEM #2588

## *IMPORTANT INTERNET SITES*

**TRADERS' LIBRARY BOOKSTORE —** *www.traderslibrary.com,* the #1 source for trading and investment books, videos and related products.

**OMEGA RESEARCH —** *www.omegaresearch.com,* Information on Omega products, support, and solution providers. Also listing of their free seminars.

**PC QUOTE —** *www.pcquote.com,* The premier source for free quotes and charts.

**DORSEY WRIGHT —** *www.dorseywright.com,* The source for information on Point & Figure analysis and comprehensive Point & Figure charts.

**EQUITY ANALYTICS —** *www.e-analytics.com,* An excellent educational resource with extensive glossaries for technical analysis and many other topics.

**MURPHYMORRIS —** *www.murphymorris.com,* The site of Technical Analysis Gurus John Murphy and Greg Morris. A perfect site for both beginners and those more experienced in Technical Analysis

**WALL STREET DIRECTORY —** *www.wsdinc.com,* The best directory of financial sites on the web. A comprehensive source that will help you find the answers to your financial questions.

**DOW JONES SEMINARS —** *www.seminarsdowjones.com,* The site of the best technical analysis conference around. Get a speaker list, registration information and a schedule for this 20 year old conference.

**JOE KRUTSINGER —** *www.joekrut.com,* The site of the author of this book and expert system developer. Includes information on his systems with information on how to get them.

**WALL STREET DIRECTORY —** *www.wsdinc.com,* The best directory of financial sites on the web. A comprehensive source that will help you find the answers to your financial questions.

**FUTURES TRUTH —** *www.futurestruth.com,* Independantly tracks hundreds of publicly available commodity trading systems.

**FUTURES MAGAZINE —** *www.futuresmag.com,* Filled with information for futures traders as well as books, videos, and information about their conferences.

**To order, see next page**

# BailSuite

How would you like to be able to trade
the futures market in a disciplined,
mechanical way **WITHOUT** investing in
software, computers, data feeds, exchange fees
or more than 5 minutes per day, per market?

## One Contract traded, $55 commission
## 08/15/95-08/15/98 Simulation Only!

| Market | Mos. Net | Max DD | # of Trades | Avg Trade | Avg # Mo. | % Right | JK Ratio | Mo Net | MMStop |
|--------|----------|--------|-------------|-----------|-----------|---------|----------|--------|--------|
| Soybeans | 36 | $ 26,335.00 | $ (4,202.00) | 173 | $152.23 | 4.81 | 60.00% | 6.27 | $731.53 | $875.00 |
| Bellies | 36 | $ 25,942.00 | $ (3,721.00) | 266 | $97.53 | 7.39 | 61.00% | 6.97 | $720.61 | $400.00 |
| Bonds | 36 | $ 34,277.00 | $ (4,418.00) | 187 | $183.30 | 5.19 | 50.00% | 7.76 | $952.14 | $531.25 |
| Coffee | 36 | $114,450.00 | $(11,633.00) | 213 | $537.32 | 5.92 | 51.00% | 9.84 | $3,179.17 | $900.00 |
| Nat Gas | 36 | $ 72,055.00 | $ (6,055.00) | 255 | $282.57 | 7.08 | 45.00% | 11.90 | $2,001.53 | $400.00 |
| NYSE | 36 | $122,275.00 | $ (9,415.00) | 235 | $520.32 | 6.53 | 48.00% | 12.99 | $3,396.53 | $750.00 |
| Wheat | 36 | $ 25,691.25 | $ (4,925.00) | 243 | $105.73 | 6.74 | 49.00% | 5.21 | $713.63 | $550.00 |
| E-Mini | 36 | $ 21,720.00 | $ (2590.00) | 325 | $66.83 | 9.00 | 42.00% | 8.38 | $603.33 | $175.00 |
| Total | | $442,745.25 | | 1897 | $243.23 | 52.66 | | | $12,298.47 | |
| IBM | 36 | $129.45 | $(10.50) | 204 | $ 0.63 | 5.67 | 66.00% | 12.33 | $3.60 | none |

( 1 share- no stops, no commissions-Free Bonus System with all orders!)

# BAIL SUITE ORDER FORM

## To get started just call **800-272-2855 ext T184**
## or 410-964-0026 ext T184
## or FAX the following form to 410-964-0027.

Name:________________________________________

Address:______________________________________

City:________________________State:____Zip:__________

Phone:__________________Fax:__________________

EMail:________________________________________

❒ MasterCard — ❒ Visa

Card Number:_____________________________Exp Date:_____

Signature ________________________________________

TradeStation Block Number:______________________________

Make checks payable to Traders' Library.

**Mail Orders To:**
**Traders' Library**
**PO BOX 2466**
**Ellicott City MD 21041**

## Check the Modules You Wish for $1250 each:

- ❒ JK1 Daily Soybeans
- ❒ JK2 Daily Pork Bellies
- ❒ JK3 Day Session Bonds
- ❒ JK4 Daily Coffee
- ❒ JK5 Daily Nat. Gas
- ❒ JK6 Day Session NYSE
- ❒ JK7 Daily Wheat
- ❒ JK8 Day E-Mini
- ☑ JK9 Daily IBM Stocks—**FREE** - with All Orders

## or

❒ YES! Send me all of Joe's trading systems described on page 91, plus a FREE IBM Stock Trading System, for just $4000.

❒ I have no TradeStation™ - send me the JK RuleSet™ instead, for all Joe's systems, for just $4,000.

*Orders will be processed by Joe Krutsinger, Inc*

# ABOUT THE AUTHOR

Joe Krutsinger, a 20 year veteran of the futures business, is President of the consulting firm, Joe Krutsinger, Inc. Joe has been recognized as one of the world's most prolific trading system developers, and was previously Vice President of Research at the futures brokerage firm, Robbins Trading Company. In addition, he has constructed commodity trading systems over the years for his own clients, as well as for some of the industry's most prominent and successful traders.

Joe has also authored two highly acclaimed books on trading systems, and has revealed some of his most powerful systems and methods at various trading seminars and conferences worldwide. Now, with the introduction of his "Bail Suite" program, the unique trading systems he has developed for 8 markets are available to the public on disk, or as a rule set, at a very special price.

## NOTES

# NOTES

## NOTES

# NOTES